Gender and History
in Medieval English
Romance and Chronicle

Studies in the Humanities
Literature—Politics—Society

Guy Mermier
General Editor

Vol. 63

PETER LANG
New York • Washington, D.C./Baltimore • Bern
Frankfurt am Main • Berlin • Brussels • Vienna • Oxford

Laura D. Barefield

Gender and History in Medieval English Romance and Chronicle

PETER LANG
New York • Washington, D.C./Baltimore • Bern
Frankfurt am Main • Berlin • Brussels • Vienna • Oxford

Library of Congress Cataloging-in-Publication Data

Barefield, Laura D.
Gender and history in medieval English
romance and chronicle / Laura D. Barefield.
p. cm. — (Studies in the humanities; v. 63)
Includes bibliographical references and index.
1. Romances, English—History and criticism. 2. English prose literature—
Middle English, 1100–1500—History and criticism. 3. Geoffrey, of
Monmouth, Bishop of St. Asaph, 1100?–1154. Historia regum Britanniae.
4. Literature and history—Great Britain—History—To 1500.
5. Historiography—Great Britain—History—To 1500. 6. Great Britain—
History—To 1485—Historiography. 7. Sex role in literature. 8. Women in
literature. I. Title. II. Studies in the humanities (New York, N.Y.); v.63.
PR321 .B35   823'.109—dc21   2002030150
ISBN 0-8204-6184-9
ISSN 0742-6712

Die Deutsche Bibliothek-CIP-Einheitsaufnahme

Barefield, Laura D.
Gender and history in medieval English
romance and chronicle / Laura D. Barefield.
–New York; Washington, D.C./Baltimore; Bern;
Frankfurt am Main; Berlin; Brussels; Vienna; Oxford: Lang.
(Studies in the humanities; Vol. 63)
ISBN 0-8204-6184-9

The paper in this book meets the guidelines for permanence and durability
of the Committee on Production Guidelines for Book Longevity
of the Council of Library Resources.

Peter Lang Publishing, Inc., New York
275 Seventh Avenue, 28th Floor, New York, NY 10001
www.peterlangusa.com

Printed in Germany

TABLE OF CONTENTS

ACKNOWLEDGMENTS

any of my colleagues have given valuable and timely support to my career and work as a scholar. I am grateful to: Kathleen O'Gorman of Illinois Wesleyan University; Helen T. Bennett, Ordelle Hill, Paula Kristofik, and Kevin Rahimzadeh of Eastern Kentucky University; Jeannie Judge, Mary Kramer, Melissa Pennell, William Roberts, and Anthony Szczesiul of the University of Massachusetts at Lowell. Special thanks go to Mary Kramer for enthusiastically proofreading the final manuscript. I very much appreciate the mentoring and support of Peggy McCracken of the University of Michigan-Ann Arbor.

I am thankful for a Provost's Grant and a Healey Grant I received from the University of Massachusetts-Lowell which helped support the research and publication of this book. I am also grateful for permission to include material in chapter two which has appeared in *Medieval Perspectives* and *Medieval Feminist Forum* and chapter one in the *Publications of the Medieval Association of the Midwest.*

I would also like to thank friends who have read, listened, and provided camaraderie in matters academic and not: Sarah Elbert, Tim Houlihan, Kari Kalve, Le Jane Liebhart, Pamela Riney-Kehrberg, Francesca Sawaya, and Judith Steinbach.

I appreciate the good cheer and hospitality that Jane Church Pierson has given me over the years. Most important thanks go to Michael Pierson, who has shared with me his love for history and everything else.

Medieval Genres: Combining the Study of Historiography and Romance

odern culture draws a clear distinction between the categories of fiction and history The post-Romantic notion of the creator-poet makes fiction the original work of an imaginative force. The writing of history requires systematic research to ascertain the veracity of real events before recounting them in narrative form or analyzing the data. In the later European Middle Ages, however, different conceptions of narrative were at work. Verse romance existed in the same courtly milieu as prose historiography—both recounted stories of the past, be they legendary material from Trojan or Arthurian cycles, Biblical episodes, or what we might call the historical material of classical Rome and Greece. In the Middle Ages, "history" was considered not as some independently verifiable record of the events that actually occurred, but as an account of past events that was authoritative, based on previous accounts. Or as some have put it, history was "what was held to be true." Thus texts that dealt with the past often held some tension between their own current versions and other accounts to which they referred. For example, Geoffrey of Monmouth and other historians often refer to several different versions of an event without evaluating their accuracy as modern historians might, or explain that they cannot know about a particular event because tradition or their antecedents do not tell them. Poetic texts share this characteristic, with Chaucer often bemoaning what his books omit and characterizing his stories as coming from many somewhat contradictory sources. Both genres strove for an authoritative presentation of the European past—retelling versions of stories told many times before, and citing the textual traditions in which they participated. However, narratives in these genres are imaginative as well, foregrounding different issues or giving more coverage to selected events.

Literary criticism has generally given most importance to the study of poetry, or in its formation of a canon for a given historical period, privileged certain genres or great authors. Thus for the British Middle Ages, Geoffrey Chaucer becomes the poet, and high, courtly romance the genre to be held up and studied as great art. But the prose historiography of this period enjoyed a popularity with medieval audiences that equaled that of medieval romance or any work of Chaucer. Romance, in fact, partook in a dual tradition with historiography.[1] Medieval histories, such as Geoffrey of Monmouth's *Historia regum Britanniae*, provided the source material for romances, while at the same time existing in a living history of textual redaction with those romances.

Just as literary critics have neglected investigating the nature of historiography as an important fictive genre in the Middle Ages, they have also neglected the interaction between these genres. Each genre has been studied separately from the other, with historiography, like the *chanson de geste*, associated with recording great deeds of great men and with celebrating nationalism, and romance associated with the emergence of the individual[2] through a test by ordeal or a quest. Romance has been seen as a genre that creates norms of chivalric behavior for knights as well as for ladies of the court. As a genre, in fact, romance is often perceived as written for a female audience,[3] while history is associated with clerical authors, writing for the education in military strategy of noble young men. One of the aims of this book will be to demonstrate that this gendered split between these genres is too simplistic. By examining the gender politics of literary patronage we find that women both read and participated in the production of historiography for courtly audiences and that the portrayal of men and women in these texts reflects this participation. Both genres explore and contribute to changes and tensions in the emerging and contradictory sex/gender system of late-medieval England; changes in genre and gender accompany and are implicated in political, institutional, and economic changes. In such a period of change, texts in both the chronicle and romance traditions provided sites that could transmit social ideologies to their readers, but that could also encourage resistance on the part of these participants in the processes of textual culture.[4]

We can explore these changes by examining both popular chronicles and romances in their social context. In particular, we will assess how certain stories change over time in response to changes in the circumstances of production from the twelfth through early-fifteenth centuries. This study will treat chronicles and romances that have elements of both, focusing especially on genealogical material. The first chapter examines Geoffrey of Monmouth's twelfth-century legendary history, the *Historia regum Britanniae*, or *History of the British Kings*, one of the most influential texts in European literary history until the seventeenth century. Subsequent chapters will move on to other works in this tradition, such as the Anglo-Norman chronicle, *Les Cronicles*, written in the early fourteenth century by Nicholas Trevet, a noted Dominican scholar, for the royal family at the behest of Mary of Woodstock, a daughter of Edward I. Linked to this chronicle is Geoffrey Chaucer's *Man of Law's Tale*, a hagiographic romance derived from it later in the century. Finally, the study turns to the anonymous Middle English chronicles produced around 1400 and known collectively as the prose *Brut*; the chapter analyzes it in tandem with the contemporary romance masterpiece, *Gawain and the Green Knight*.

Parataxis, Genealogy, and Readers

As a rule, medieval historical narrative is far more paratactic than its more modern counterparts. One way that scholars have considered parataxis is as a marker of oral culture, with subordination marking more advanced, more literate and analytical ways of arranging and thinking about material.[5] More recently, however, this model has become more complicated, with Brian Stock positing a complex interplay between literate and oral practice rather than a model of emerging literacy. In medieval French culture, he finds different kinds of literacy that exist within the play of different language communities and within different institutions such as church and state, each wielding cultural power through the texts they produced.[6]

These rhetorical styles, parataxis, or coordination, and hypotaxis, or subordination, thus may serve to mark the play of power relations in a text. In medieval histories, which are predominantly paratactic, sections of subordinate narratives may mark literate sophistication, but scholars also identify them as romance elements. What has gone unremarked, and what this study will examine as its major focus, is that gendered moments often mark these spaces where the subordinate narrative breaks off from the larger paratactic framework, creating a rhetorical space between history and romance that marks social and political power undergoing a process of negotiation.[7]

 By examining how parataxis and hypotaxis function in the high courtly genres of chronicle and romance, we find that the process by which these texts branch from one style into the other and back again are key places for the deployment and construction of gender, often through opposition, and usually situated in narratives of national or cultural crisis. By tracing how paratactic genealogy structures these texts, but also how gendered moments break this pattern and turn the text toward subordinate stories, typically characterized as more literate, analytical, or romantic, we can begin to chart how authors took advantage of these moments to create aspects of their culture's sex/gender system, and how they, as well as readers, used these sites to resist or recreate aspects of those systems.

While the appeal of medieval history's paratactic construction can be lost to modern readers—for we are accustomed to waiting for the conclusion or resolution—these seemingly endless, sequential texts found great favor with medieval readers. Manuscripts abound in great numbers, and in the twelfth century, translating histories from Latin into the vernacular became a growth industry which would last well into the Renaissance. The prominence of these texts in early European culture leads us to ask how these narratives are put together and how they can make meaning when they include so very few logical connectives, usually only chronological or sequential markers, such as "and" or "then."

Hayden White argues that sequence in medieval histories is a form of signification unto itself. In analyzing the barest of annals, merely a list of years beside some of which are listed events written in spare syntax, White finds that the passing of each year in textual form creates a principle of continuity and even plentitude. In contrast to the scarcity suggested by the accounts of famine, flood, and war, the annal form shows "no scarcity of the years: they descend regularly from their origin, the year of the Incarnation, and roll relentlessly on to their potential end, the last Judgement." In this way, "the narrative strains for the effect of having filled in all the gaps, of having put an image of continuity, coherency and meaning in place of the fantasies of emptiness, need, and frustrated desire that inhabit our nightmares about the destructive power of time."[8] Medieval chronicles are a more complex form than the bare annal, but in spite of their narrative voices' occasional motions toward closure, interpretation, or subordination, they retain chronology and the coordinate, seemingly unending sameness of the sequential passing of years as their basic structure. Their stylistic complexity seems a mark of the kind of textual community in conflict among different types of discourse, both oral and written, with their accompanying tensions among the power of social groups involved in the textual process.

The gaps and lack of explicit logical connectives in such a paratactic narrative structure which are so apparent and frustrating to modern readers may not have been apparent to medieval ones.[9] Yet historical narratives work hard to achieve the effect of continuity. This book will argue that this effort is not always successful in medieval chronicle and that gaps and slippages in chronology and coordination provide opportunities for readers and for writers to counter the seemingly natural discourse of continuity and history to fill their own personal and political needs.

Yet how can continuity emerge from narratives that are often choppy, with coordinate structure, and no explicit connection between their parts? The connection between the parts of a genealogical list are often completely unexpressed syntactically. Genealogy, therefore, offers a good focus for studying chronicle, romance, and their conceptions of the past, since this narrative style can structure both genres and indeed is a mark of their generic intermediacy. Medieval readers must have recognized the gaps in the sequence and actively participated in providing them with meaning. Gabrielle Speigel comments that "genealogy overcomes the conceptual parataxis suggested by medieval narrative form" and that "if the chronicler's matter was not explicitly linked by a syntax of relation there is no reason to assume that a medieval reader could not have made the necessary connections in his own mind."[10] White gives a further example of this reading phenomenon: "1056: The Emperor Henry died and his son Henry succeeded to the rule." He observes that the connection between the sequence is ambiguous and only "achieves closure by its tacit invocation of the legal system, the rule of genealogical succession which the annalist takes for granted as a principle rightly governing the passing of authority from one generation to another."[11] A reader thus must forge a connection between the syntactic parts by reference to the social system of which he or she is a part, including the contemporary sex/gender system.[12] By repetitively staging the passing of human generations, the paratactic text implicates readers, making them participants in this social process. Medieval audiences, through their readings of the fantastic events of romance and chronicle which were nonetheless considered historical, engaged in a process of producing the past and of producing themselves as historical subjects.

In twelfth-century England and France, genealogical narratives were very common throughout different kinds of texts, and representations of generations of families permeated secular and religious life.[13] The way people thought about what constituted family, that is, the network of people to whom they were related, was also changing under pressures economic, religious, and political. Georges Duby first charts these tensions in conceptions of lineage in northern France, arguing that as a single heir begins to take prominence in inheritance practices, genealogies become more hierarchical, foregrounding a system of patriarchs and heirs that extends backward in time to a founder of the line, and thereby displacing an earlier kinship system that stressed contemporary, lateral connections among both male and female sides of a family.[14] David Herlihy complicates Duby's findings and argues that one system of reckoning kinship did not simply replace the other, but that both systems, one privileging patriarchal status, and the other leaving space for women's familial connections, compete for dominance.[15] We thus find inheritance practice, with its accompanying conceptions of genealogical succession and lineage, to be quite varied in this period, from Geoffrey of Monmouth's first writing of British history to its last medieval redaction in the prose *Brut*.

In Britain, these crises of succession and lineage were particularly murky. Questions of who could inherit and how a line could be traced were particularly pertinent to a culture engaged in a civil war between its king, Stephen, the nephew of the previous monarch, Henry I, and Matilda, the daughter of that monarch, whose father had sworn his nobles to uphold her rights as his heir. These questions continued as Henry Plantagenet and his line took over British rule based on his mother's connection as Henry I's only remaining, legitimate offspring. Primogeniture was the standard Norman practice by this period, but in England after the Conquest, a lack of clear male succession compelled the Normans to designate their heirs until the reign of Henry II.[16] The difficulty of establishing and maintaining a single, legitimate, and competent male line to inherit the family fortunes was far from extraordinary in Anglo-Norman culture. Their emerging economic and political institutions, as well as texts they produced, betray the cultural tension and fascination arising from the hotly contested issues of female heirs, suitable mothers, legitimacy of birth, and conflicts between heirs. This concern with lineage filtered through all levels of the English aristocracy, since the only way to press a claim for land was to claim inheritance and to be able to prove relation, creating a noble class whose membership was fluid.[17]

In these circumstances, British rulers used their genealogies to shape the British past and create a history that installed them legitimately as kings, both as eldest sons, but also through disputed female lines. Texts created legendary founders and divine origins for Britain as a way to provide continuity for the royal line. Although they present the Trojan and Arthurian origins of Britain as unproblematic, these narratives subvert the stability of that origin by playing out its generational action through conflict. These story patterns question the very linearity of historical narrative itself and particularly their political aims. These texts embody crises of heritability: they face the difficulties of creating new lineage and of how sex and gender can regulate an economy, its politics, and its culture. Behind an author's choice of a genealogical narrative structure lie important assumptions about gender and how filial succession can structure the shape of reality.

Genealogy can become even further mythologized, creating a narrative *mythos*, a symbolic form for the past; events from the past become emplotted as genealogy, just as traditional forms such as biographical portraits and *gestes* become linked by the principle of succession. Because this narrative model is filiative, procreation becomes a metaphor for historical change. Such history based on recording people's ties to a mythic origin replicates Christian generative myths with "creation" becoming the law that orders community. Thus the promulgation of genealogical history, in its repetition of lineage after lineage, naturalizes and embeds patriarchy and the assumptions concerning gender it brings within the text's narrative structure.[18]

Naturalizing patriarchy as a system demands a smoothly flowing genealogical narration—if kings beget true, that is legitimate, and even competent sons to take over the reins of government smoothly, society is represented as stable and the system which rules it as unproblematic. This form, however, has very narrow requirements. The son, the object of the first clause, is transformed into a new father, the subject of the next clause, and in order to meet these requirements, it must cut out or suppress other political and narrative possibilities such as multiple sons or female heirs. Genealogy, a form whose subject is the production of generations, can often elide the place occupied by women both in the politics of succession and in the processes of reproduction itself. In order to naturalize patriarchal succession, genealogies often try to usurp this reproductive, female authority by suppressing female figures.[19]

If genealogy makes procreation a metaphor for historical change, it is a metaphor that has been masculinized by this narrative form because the pivotal roles that women play can be concealed or usurped by most genealogical moments. Submerging women's roles can be integral to a text's rhetorical strategy: the smooth passing of generations, the accomplishment of narrative itself and the creation of patriarchy. At critical moments of the text, when parataxis is broken by subordinate stories, linear genealogy and the emerging system of patriarchal succession it narrates, intersects in complex ways with systems of marriage practice that furnish brides to families to be mothers of their next generations. Motherhood creates a position for women from which they can create signs, but there is no single meaning for women in this dynamic.[20] Figures of women and their narrative, therefore, can draw all variety of social tensions about difference and resulting social conflicts.

For aristocratic culture, the proper succession of stability and power depended on women's bodily integrity, and so medieval women's political power can be grounded by their role in the succession. Eleanor of Aquitaine serves as an example of a woman who achieved political power in a complex and contradictory way—she was accused of adultery, yet her production of three daughters and five sons gave her huge political power in the court of Henry II, as well as in Anglo-French relations at large. Her case demonstrates that the actions of women had "potentially disruptive and violent consequences for the orderly succession that her position was intended to guarantee."[21]

In medieval chronicles and the texts derived from them, women are essential to the production of story and of text. At a minimum, they are often literally included in the paradigms of succession, for example, "the king had a son by his queen." In this way, their necessity to dynastic succession is acknowledged, but once included in the text, women gain authority in a variety of ways. They enable the narration of patriarchy; thus, their actions can also easily destroy it, and they show how fragile and contingent such a vision of history and so-cial stability may be.

This study explores the complex interfaces between gender and genres in late medieval British culture. By juxtaposing the study of selected chronicles and romances, it will unearth new possibilities for how gender ideology was constructed in this pivotal period when Saxon culture was gradually overlaid by Norman politics and eco-nomic practices, when Anglo-Saxon became Middle English, when French was spoken in the British Isles, and when Latin was the au-thoritative language of religion. Gender in romance has been well-studied, but never in connection with a genre like the British chroni-cles. Studying their similar agendas and similar production context will throw into new relief the cultural concerns addressed by both courtly narratives as they reproduced stories about the generations of Britain's past.

Gender, Genealogy, and the Politics of Succession in Geoffrey of Monmouth's *Historia regum Britanniae*

he problem of genre has always been a central issue for scholarship concerning the *Historia regum Britanniae*. Historians, while sometimes acknowledging the existence of a genre called "legendary history," often react defensively to medieval historiography as a whole, and most particularly to Geoffrey of Monmouth's text.[1] To a discipline that in its modern incarnation continues to concern itself with questions of evidence, the capacity of medieval histories for recording fantastic events or ones which are clearly disproven by other sources, at best presents an embarrassment and at worst, poses a threat to the validity of history as a field of inquiry. Many historians would agree that "Geoffrey was a romance writer masquerading as a historian. No historian today would object to him if he had avowedly written a historical novel...or a romance epic. But on the contrary, he pretended to be writing history."[2]

The reputation of the *Historia regum Britanniae* has been salvaged by literary scholars. Some critics have examined not only the subsequent influence of the history on European texts,[3] but have also probed philosophical,[4] and political issues.[5] Other critics have recently embraced more theoretical approaches, including post-colonial, feminist, and psychoanalytically-based readings.[6]

By exploring such aspects, the work of literary critics has done much to recoup the reputation of a writer who was popular throughout the Middle Ages. When the criticism is viewed along with historians' rejection of the *Historia regum Britanniae*, however, we find that scholarship from both fields has neglected inquiry into the historiographic character of the narrative.[7] The *Historia regum Britanniae* is strictly chronological and genealogical in its organizational structure. Its style is predominantly paratactic, consisting of long strings of coordinate syntax, with incidents only loosely linked by coordinating or sequential conjunctions. This pattern is regularly broken by digressions into subordinate stories, but even after the long Arthurian narrative at its center, the *Historia regum Britanniae* always returns to a strict, chronological listing of the generations of kings. History is no masquerade for Geoffrey of Monmouth. The most notable and defining structural and stylistic elements of his narrative are those of medieval historiography.

One way to explain the generic contradictions of the *Historia regum Britanniae* is to examine how the text served the political needs of the Plantagenets.[8] For instance, Henry II's problem was one of political legitimization, proving that he had a hereditary right to rule through his mother Matilda's claims,[9] and he used literary and legendary texts such as the *Historia regum Britanniae* to help create his political authority. In such turbulent times, "the disruptions of medieval political history were typically healed with the soothing continuities of a founding legend, and insecure rulers bolstered their regimes by invoking honorific if legendary precedents."[10] Part of the complexity of the *Historia regum Britanniae*, however, is that although it presents the Trojan and Arthurian origins of Britain as unproblematic, the text subverts the stability of that origin by playing out its generational action. As a Vergilian narrative that charts the destruction of empire and its re-establishment in a new place, it includes tales of parricide, internecine conflict, and infidelity. These story patterns question the very linearity of historical narrative itself, and Geoffrey embraced and exploited these contradictions. The *Historia regum Britanniae* operates at once as both legitimating and subverting the social order.

While trying to illustrate the authority of Trojan ancestry, this narrative deconstructs that origin; the *Historia* thus embodies a crisis of political succession: the difficulty of creating a new lineage from disparate peoples. Behind Geoffrey of Monmouth's choice of a genealogical narrative structure lie important assumptions about gender and how filial succession can structure the shape of "reality." Gabrielle Spiegel points out that "through the imposition of genealogical

patriarchy &
genealogical narrative

metaphors on historical narrative, genealogy becomes for historiography not only a thematic "myth" but a narrative *mythos*, a symbolic form which governs the very shape and significance of the past" and theorizes that this filiative structure, in fact, can make readers see procreation as a metaphor for historical change.[11] When a text such as Geoffrey's repeats lineage after lineage, it naturalizes and embeds patriarchy, and the assumptions concerning gender it brings, within the text's narrative structure.

The political interests of patriarchy demand a smoothly flowing genealogical narration—if kings beget true sons who take over the reins of government smoothly, society is represented as stable and the system that rules it as unproblematic. This form has very narrow requirements, however: the son, the object of the first clause, is transformed into a new father, the subject of the next clause, and in order to meet these requirements, it must cut out or suppress other political and narrative possibilities such as multiple sons or female heirs. In particular, genealogy, a form whose subject is the production of generations, often elides the place occupied by mothers in both reproduction and in the politics of succession.

If genealogy makes procreation a metaphor for historical change, it is a metaphor that has been masculinized by this narrative form because the pivotal roles that women play are concealed by most genealogical moments. Submerging women's roles can be, in fact, integral to the smooth passing of generations and the accomplishment of narrative itself.[12] Geoffrey's use of his genealogical historical form is not so simple, however. Primogeniture was not yet well-established in England, and the royal succession was contested on a number of fronts in the eleventh and early-twelfth centuries. Both William Rufus and Henry I overcame the claims of their older brother, Robert Curthose, and Matilda fought for her father's throne against her cousin, Stephen, whose claim came through his mother's family.[13] At the time of Geoffrey's writing, it was far from clear that the Plantagenet line would prevail for the next three hundred years. Exploring through a Vergilian narrative the kind of crises of reproduction found in his own post-Conquest society, Geoffrey uses the contingent nature of these narrative and political structures as an opportunity to experiment with historical form, breaking from the parataxis of genealogy to subordinate romance narratives.

Romance in the *Historia regum Britanniae* is always situated within the larger structure of genealogy, lineage, and the progress of the years of British history. Such a dual narrative allows the motives of each narrative mode, for romance, the testing of communal values[14] and for history, the creation of plenty and political validity for patriarchal society,[15] to influence the function of the other. Each genre can throw the motives of the other into relief and also open them to question. As the years of genealogical history churn on, the narrative hits snags and crises in trying to provide the appropriate heir to further the smooth and seemingly natural functioning of patriarchy. Romance narratives in the *Historia regum Britanniae* explore and often resolve these crises through examining the emerging and contested gendered systems of inheritance and succession. Because these romances are situated within the larger historical narrative, however, their recourse to the themes and concerns of historiography allows figures in the romance tales to partake of the complex and contradictory authority created by the ways men and women are positioned in lineage. In this way, the text addresses crises of reproduction, both of text and of lineage, making a new people and a new history, helping to create and explore the emerging sex/gender system of late-medieval, Northern Europe.

The generic tension within Geoffrey's text is a complex response to the politics in the medieval Britain of his day. The parataxis of genealogy allows Geoffrey to provide solace and the continuity of history and lineage, all the while using breaks in the story to explore complications in this political agenda in the more subordinate form of romance. Romance figures also benefit from their positioning within the larger narrative, creating a more complex, conflicted, and open arena for the performance of gender roles.[16]

This dual narrative form makes Geoffrey's text ideally suited for political use through generations of British and European aristocracy throughout and beyond the medieval period. By looking at how these genres work with and across one another, we see new questions of gender emerging: how paradoxical women's roles are when situated within genealogy; how foregrounding the creation of a patriarch may expose the artificiality of his lineage; what choices are forced upon women as the text dramatizes their absorption into genealogy; how difficult creating a suitable heir to the father's position can be. In communal terms, each instance of conflict interrogates the system

and probes how the narrative itself could cease. Instead of reinstitut-
ing the order of a political and social system, the text could fail to re-
peat itself, reproducing only social chaos and conflict.

Rather than shutting down or containing critical moments to gain
a smoothly proceeding chronology, the text exploits them to narrative
advantage, exploring how the gendered aspects of these crises can
both legitimate, but also question the operations of the narrative and
the patriarchal mythos it masks and re-enacts. By foregrounding gender, the *Historia regum Britanniae* probes the tensions surrounding
the creation, preservation, and transfer of textual and political power.
Through exploiting the critical moments between coordinate and
subordinate narrative, the *Historia regum Britanniae* denaturalizes its
own genealogical form, confronting both the threat and the possibilities offered by the narration of history, and perhaps even offering
members of its audiences, situated in various political contexts over
the years of its reception, positions from which to question or alter
the social system it narrates. By examining gender in this political
text, we can begin to see how popular medieval historiography, as
well as closely related romances, are determined as genres and how
their ideologies functioned.[17]

The *Historia regum Britanniae* begins with a Vergilian narrative,
telling the adventures of Brutus, a descendent of Aeneas, who leaves
Italy after inadvertently killing his parents and travels to Greece,
where he frees a band of enslaved Trojan refugees. These people sail
through European seas until they arrive in England to found the British nation. Geoffrey's text continues to narrate succeeding generations of British kings as they triumph over internal enemies and
external threats, and as they are conquered by the Romans and in-
vaded by Saxon colonists. The second half of the *Historia* is domi-
nated by the rise and fall of the British King Arthur, explaining how
he consolidated his power among the British nobles, expelled the Saxons, and ultimately conquered Rome itself before his downfall at the
hands of his traitorous bastard son Mordred. The chronicle follows a
few more generations of kings, but ends with British defeat. The next
section of this chapter will examine the generic instability of history
and romance in the narrative of Brutus's exile from Rome and the
founding of Britain, to illustrate in more detail how Geoffrey's text
uses genealogy and romance to engage with gender and the politics of
his day.

Creating Lineage: The Exile and Rehabilitation of Brutus

The *Historia regum Britanniae* is a chronicle of Britain, beginning with a geographic description of this "Britannia, insularum optima" (221)[18] reminiscent of the beginning of Bede's *Ecclesiastical History*, as well as an earlier sixth-century history by Gildas, the *De excidio et conquestu Britanniae*, and the late eighth-century *Historia Brittonum* of Nennius. Where Bede and Gildas begin their histories by explaining how the Romans under Claudius first settled the island, however, Geoffrey expands one of Nennius' origin stories to provide a legendary, explicitly Vergilian origin for his history that he says will explain whence and how the Britons first came to the island.[19] The first part of the *Historia regum Britanniae* starts where the *Aeneid* ends, beginning to explain the exploits of the generations of Aeneas, revealed in his prophetic vision in book VI of the epic and also related by Livy.[20] But the Roman generations soon become compromised: the lineage should run smoothly from Aeneas, to Ascanius, to Silvius, to Brutus. In only the second generation after Aeneas, however, the succession becomes embroiled in blood crimes that virtually destroy the paternal line. Forging a new Troy becomes an illusion when the lineage being reconstituted is taken from a mixture of Trojans, Latins, and Rutulians, and instead of creating the next generation, an act of parricide kills the one before it. Political succession becomes a textual and national crisis: neither sequence can continue without some exploration and at least partial or temporary resolution of these tensions.

As a result of this moment of crisis, the paratactic genealogy of Aeneas becomes transformed into the subordinate romance of the exile and wanderings of Brutus. By examining this tale and the circumstances that precipitate it, this chapter will demonstrate how the *Historia regum Britanniae* foregrounds the constructed and artificial nature of "lineage" and the processes by which it can be created, destroyed, and recreated, in a story that first creates a new patriarch, next finds him an appropriate wife, and finally, returns to parataxis and genealogy. The romance narrative strives to fill the gap created when the national narrative breaks down. Romance accomplishes social integration, although in an often contradictory and incomplete way, for these critical moments hinge on issues of blood and gender which are difficult to resolve and which continue to rupture the narrative.

The romance of Brutus strives to create a new, Trojan, ultimately British lineage in three ways. First, the narrative creates Brutus as a model of heroic masculinity who may then take his place as a patriarch and founder of a culture. Second, the narrative foregrounds the process by which Brutus is given a suitable wife and mother for his line,[21] in the process illustrating what kind of woman is needed for this role and the loss that assuming this position must entail for her. Last, the conclusion of the romance narrative, childbirth, literally returns the narrative to a genealogical structure. In these ways, gender relations construct the narrative, but the narrative also treats models of gendered behavior as themselves constructed, giving readers some room to negotiate and question these constructs.

The crisis of succession begins with the circumstances surrounding Brutus's birth. This early Roman history begins by describing a protracted war among the different groups of Italians, as Aeneas "regum Italie et Laviniam filiam Latini adeptus est" (223) ["seized both the kingdom of Italy and the person of Lavinia, who was the daughter of Latinus" (54)]. Through marrying Lavinia, Aeneas makes a political alliance with her father, Latinus, and assures his Trojan son, Ascanius, a kingdom to rule and his descendants a place to thrive. By creating such a dynastic marriage between the warring factions, the *Historia regum Britanniae* promises that Latins and Trojans will be united in the future, living in a stable, normalized kingdom, and that they will become a new, united people in an unproblematic kindred.

The text, however, immediately shows this marriage and the new dynasty it promises to be a false hope. Rather than two races merged into one bloodline, the generations of Aeneas illustrate that supposedly transformed bloodlines remain present. In the third generation, the marriage of Silvius excavates some of these ethnic tensions. Geoffrey writes that Silvius "furtive veneri indulgens nupsit ciudam nepti Lavinie eamque fecit pregnantem" (223) ["was involved in a secret love affair with a certain niece of Lavinia's; he married her and made her pregnant" (54)]. Silvius is still considered Trojan, a descendant of Aeneas, and the niece is marked as Latin, belonging to Lavinia's race. Lavinia's marriage to Aeneas has not fully absorbed Latinus' family into Trojan kinship networks.[22] Rather than an economic or political bargain between men, this relationship is a "furtive veneri" that is only later legitimated by marriage.[23]

Instead of providing the illusion of continued social stability and the future existence of Aeneas' line by providing a son and heir, the product of this inter-racial[24] marriage, Brutus, shows by his birth and subsequent deeds how easily the structures of family and country can be overthrown through parricide and regicide. When Ascanius, the current Roman leader, hears news of his expected grandchild, he asks soothsayers to divine its sex, illustrating his concern about whether the lineage of Aeneas, once again mixed with Lavinia's ancestry, will be successfully united in a male child who could then succeed his father and grandfather. Half of these hopes are fulfilled: the child will perpetuate the mixed lineage of the Trojans and the Latins. But the birth of Brutus transgresses the political needs of patriarchal society and the historical narrative that seeks to legitimate it. The delivery of this hoped-for heir kills his mother, and he later accidentally kills his father, Silvius, with an arrow during a hunt. The early setting of the *Historia regum Britanniae* promises to continue the Vergilian schema of the generations of Rome, but the blood crimes of Brutus, coming immediately after the interethnic union of his mother and father, derail the genealogical narrative.

It has certainly been the hope of traditional views of historical texts like the *Historia regum Britanniae* that recovery will follow loss and that "new orders" can be free of the violence of the past.[25] These texts themselves, however, acknowledge that even the newly established society will face inevitable violence and fall—for instance, at the end of the *Aeneid*, instead of granting mercy, Aeneas kills Turnus because he sees him wearing the belt of his slaughtered young comrade, Pallas. In the "loss and recovery" interpretation of epic and historical narratives, however, we find too easy an acceptance of a kind of patriarchal optimism espoused by the texts, that through heroic endeavor past horrors can somehow finally be obliterated and that the present and future can offer peaceful stasis, or at least an affirmation of society's valiant efforts to save itself. I would argue that the *Historia regum Britanniae*'s repetitive narrative is not simply the tragedy of civilization, but that the alternation between genealogy and romance illustrates how this paradigm is grounded upon tensions in conceptions of gender and family.

Because the blood crimes surrounding Brutus's life in Rome violate the mythic promise of empire, he is made an exile by the very family group he has threatened, by his own "indignantibus parentes", or angry relatives, who expel him from his Italian homeland because he had committed "tantum facinus" (224), such a great crime. When

Brutus arrives in Greece, he is effectively a man who has cut off his own family ties, a man without lineage. In the wars that follow, in which Brutus leads the Greek branch of Trojans against their Greek king, Pandrasus, he not only creates himself as a masculine hero, but also erases his legacy of parricide by identifying himself with the Trojan lineage of his great-grandfather, Aeneas. He becomes a Trojan anew to lead Trojans out of bondage.

Brutus's attainment of a specific type of heroic masculinity is achieved by the text's recognition of and praise for his military prowess, as well as by the detailed narration of his violent military campaigns. Louise Fradenburg has pointed out that such violent military narratives are part of the cultural work that historical texts perform. By insisting repetitively that men prove themselves in the test of combat, such a text produces "glory" through a cycle of loss and sacrifice. By creating such masculine heroes, "history incites men to glory, to sacrifice" and this process promises to save culture.[26] In his first short portrait of a good leader, Geoffrey's description of Brutus's praiseworthy qualities participates in this process:

> In tantum autem militia & probitate vigere cepit. Ita ut regibus & principibus pre omni iuventute patrie amareture. Erat enim inter sapientes sapiens inter bellicosos bellicosus & quicquid auri vel argenti sive ornamentorum adquirebat totum militibus erogabat. Divulgata itaque peruniversas nationes ipsius fama (224–25)

> [He soon gained such fame for his military skill and prowess that he was esteemed by the kings and princes more than any young man in the country. Among the wise, he was most wise and among the valiant, he too was most valiant. All the gold and silver which he acquired he handed over to his soldiers. In this way, his fame spread among all peoples. (55)].

Brutus's characterization depends upon "militia" and "probitate", but his renown for these virtues depends upon them being recognized and hence created by specific groups—his peers, the "reges" and "principes," his soldiers, and the enslaved Trojans who later ask him to lead them. Although these qualities are conventional ones, in order for Brutus to be heroically masculine, they must be represented as exemplary. Brutus is the superlative hero, "inter sapientes sapiens" and "inter bellicosos bellicosus" and he is known for these attributes more than any other young man. The exile and pariah becomes the epitome of the noble and brave, yet wise and generous, young, male leader.

Once the text has established Brutus's reputation, the accounts of his violent campaigns to free the Trojans in Greece, as well as his later forays in France and Britain, reiterate and continually re-create these military qualities. His first battle against the Greek king, Pandrasus, particularly shows his violent skill: he ambushes the unarmed Greeks as they pass by his hidden forces, creating chaos as his forces "stagem ingerere nitumtur" (227) ["press forward to a massacre"]. After driving the Greeks into a nearby river, Brutus's fighting takes center stage with the kind of balanced rhetoric and activity that makes his killing force as all-pervasive as Achilles fighting the river Scamander in the *Iliad*: "Quos diffugientes Brutus infest: infestatos vero partim in undis partim super ripam prosternit et nunc hac nunc illac discurrans, duplicem necem ipsis ingestam esse letatur" (227–28) [as the Greeks flee, Brutus kills them on the bank and in the river. He runs now here, now there]. The strands of action are brought together in a phrase; this scene is a "duplicem necem," a double death which the text says gave Brutus "ingestam," great pleasure, as he killed his foes in this way. In his next foray, Brutus shows the same skill for brilliant strategy, laying siege to Pandrasus' camp, leading a stealthful night attack, and capturing the Greek king. When his forces spend the night in slaughter, the result (igitur) is that Brutus is again "maximo gaudio fluctuans" (233) [raging with the greatest joy]. Brutus's military virtues are grounded in detailed, violent moments such as these. In the midst of his slaughter, he can take a kind of pleasure that is the foundation of a mythic, militarized masculinity.

Brutus himself does not die in battle, although others of his supporters do in brief narratives that showcase their valiant deaths.[27] By coming through all his struggles alive, with his virtues and reputation intact, he becomes the kind of proven hero who is eligible for patriarch status, reproducing his line and establishing a new home for his Trojans in England. In the act of memorializing a hero such as Brutus, historical texts not only create a violent model of masculinity, but they also hold it up to be followed by their readers.[28] The *Historia regum Britanniae* does not participate in this process uncritically, however, for I would argue that its continual undercutting and re-instituting of its narrative and heroes allows those readers to perceive its contingent and contradictory nature.

The creation of Brutus's heroic masculinity gradually constructs his place within the recreated lineage of Troy. This context makes

him not just a young hero, but a patriarch in the making within a genealogy stretching back to ancient Trojan lords as well as looking
forward to the promise of some future empire with equally famous
leaders such as King Arthur.[29]

Brutus begins to count himself a Trojan when he comes upon the
community of enslaved Trojans in Greece. Exiled by his own family
in Italy "agnita igitur veterum prosapia moratus est Brutus apud eos"
(225) [Brutus recognized the lineage of his ancestors, and therefore
stayed among them]. Common lineage draws Brutus to these people.
Rome has rejected him, and so he goes back beyond the generations of
the immediate past that he has wronged to that of Trojan Aeneas. He
explicitly takes this lineage when he declares war against Pandrasus
as he claims that he is "dux reliquiarum Troie" (226) [the leader of the
remnants of Troy] and when he further characterizes his people's
lineage as "preclaro genere Dardani" [from the famous line of Darda-
nus].

Society as a whole begins to recognize Brutus's claim to noble
Trojan lineage. After Brutus captures Pandrasus, the Greek king acknowledges his military prowess and explicitly ties it to his famous
lineage, calling him "probitas adolescenti" (236), and skipping his
grandfather Aeneas, praises him as the heir of even older Trojan patriarchs. He submits to Brutus in a long pangyric that marks out the
hero's new social status. He calls him a young man

> quem ex genere Priami & Anchise creatum & nobilitas quae in ipso pu-
> lulat & fama nobis cognita declarat. Quis etenim alter exules Troiae in
> servitutem tot & tantorum principum positos eorundem vinculis
> eriperet. Quis cum illis regi Grecorum resisteret aut cum tam paucis tan-
> tam armatorum copiam prelio provocaret initoque conressu regem
> eorum vinctum duceret? (236)

> [whose nobility, which flourishes in him, and his fame, which is well
> known to us, show him to be of the true race of Priam and Anchises.
> Who other but he could have freed from their chains the exiles of Troy,
> when they were enslaved by so many mighty princes? Who other but he
> could have led them in their resistance to the King of the Greeks; or have
> challenged in battle such a vast concourse of warriors with so few men,
> and led their King in chains in the very first engagement? (Thorpe 57)]

Such social recognition and validation show the recovery of Brutus
from a state of exile and from the crime of parricide. Not only is society giving him sanction, it is making him a hero to be held up as a

model. As Pandrasus reiterates, who else, what other young man could have done what Brutus has done?

This social recognition is an integral part of Brutus's recouping his lineage and his heroic status, and it is also part of the reward he gains for having undergone such a violent sequence of events. Pandrasus does not just submit to Brutus; his speech gives Brutus the status of not only an equal in nobility, but an heir to his kingdom by making him his son-in-law. As a result ("ergo") of his achievements, his character, and his success in resisting Greek power, Pandrasus says "Do ei filiam mean Innogen. Do etiam aurum & argentum" (236) [I give to him my daughter Ignoge. I also give gold and silver]. He also promises to give Brutus a third of his kingdom if he remains in Greece or to give him ships and provisions if he wishes to leave. Through this settlement, Brutus gains access to political power in a legitimate way. If he succeeds Pandrasus, he will supplant him in a way that should promise continuity and the stability of patriarchy, as opposed to his earlier killing of his own father.

Brutus has begun the process of becoming a hero and generating his own lineage. Women, however, hitherto nearly absent in the narrative, now begin to play a pivotal role, showing how the creation of patriarchy coerces or demands their consent. In the figure of Ignoge, the narrative examines what kind of female figure would enable the generational schema to function and recreate itself with a new lineage. A marriage between Brutus and Ignoge promises peaceful co-existence and the mixing of two races, the Greeks and the Trojans. An exogamous marriage such as this, or as Rubin would call it, the gift of a woman, "is more profound than the result of other gift transactions because the relationship thus established is not just one of reciprocity, but one of kinship. The exchange partners have become affines and their descendants will be related by blood" (173). Both men, in this case Pandrasus and Brutus, linked by a traded woman, have a stake in maintaining the social order which will give them political and economic power. This promise of shared power and social stability, however, is immediately undercut by the *Historia regum Britanniae*.

Such a dynastic marriage, of course, opened the *Historia regum Britanniae*: the marriage between Aeneas and Lavinia, with the tensions surrounding the co-existence of their early descendants. Although the marriage of Brutus and Ignoge may promise stability, one of Brutus's Trojan followers points out the tensions and unrealistic expectations involved in assuming that a marriage is all it takes to assure peaceful co-existence. Mempricus argues that if

> partem Greciae adepti inter Danaos manere velitis numquam diuturna pace fruemini dum fratres & fillii & nepotes eorum quibus aeternam intulistis stragem vobis vel inmixit vel vincini fuerint. Semper enim necis parentum suorum memores aeterno vos habebunt odio. Quibus que etiam nugis incitati vindictam sumere nitentur" (234)

> [you wish to occupy a part of Greece and remain there among the descendants of Danaus, you will never enjoy lasting peace as long as the brother, sons, and grandsons of those on whom you have inflicted decisive defeat remain intermingled with you or as your neighbors. They will always remember the slaughter of their relatives and they will hate you forever. They will take offense for the merest trifles and they will do all in their power to take vengeance (62)].

The memories of the members of one lineage will feed memory of the conflict, and in spite of a marriage between Brutus and Pandrasus's daughter, Ignoge, the chances that two races can successfully comingle are slim, because of the very warrior culture which not only creates new heroes such as Brutus, but also remembers the deeds of past heroes. The solution that Membritius poses to this problem is to maintain the integrity of Trojan blood and to travel to a new place where the Trojans can hold the upper hand of political power, without the threat of an historical counter memory held by a vanquished foe.[30]

The *Historia regum Britanniae* also destabilizes Brutus's settlement by exposing its dependence on specific models of gender. Brutus may claim Trojan descent through his father, Silvius, but his mother was clearly a Latin. The three sons who are later born to him and Ignoge are also seen as heirs to a Trojan legacy. The mixing in these unions points to an interesting social and mythic process—a hero like Brutus can marry a woman of a different nationality such as Ignoge to gain political alliances and to conclude the war with the Greeks. But in order for Brutus's people to claim the privileged genealogy of "Trojanness" for their progeny and become the wandering people who ultimately establish Britain, Ignoge's family ties must be obliterated from the genealogical and historical record. As the *Historia* represents this contradiction, women possess blood ties for the purposes of marriage and political alliance, but do not in terms of subsequent accountings of lineage. Brutus's Trojan people are quite a mixed race of

Trojan, Latin, and Greek, but this history creates a myth of Trojan identity by submerging the blood ties borne by women and privileging the family line borne by the men.[31]

This progression of patriarchal lineage thus also becomes the moment of female loss, the moment when the woman who has entered a dynastic marriage faces the erasure of her own lineage and racial identity. When the Trojans sail away from Greece, Geoffrey writes

> At Innogen in excelsa puppi stans inter brachia Brutusi in extasi collabitur. Fusisque cum singulti lacrimis parentes ac patriam deserere conqueritur. Nex oculos a litore avertit dum litora oculis patuerunt (237)

> [Ignoge stood on the deck and from time to time fell fainting in the arms of Brutus. She wept and sobbed at being forced to leave her relations and her homeland; and as long as the shore lay there before her eyes, she would not turn her gaze away from it (64)].

The concern here is explicit; Ignoge is leaving her "Greekness" behind in the form of both family and country and must face being absorbed into this Trojan dynastic venture. Critics have interpreted this extended treatment as merely an example of pathos. For instance, Robert Hanning describes pathetic moments in the *Historia regum Britanniae* as involving a "bystander or helpless victim of national crisis" and observes that "all are women." Of Ignoge's lament, he writes that "history is forgotten and attention is focused on the timeless problem of wives and lovers."[32] History, however, is not forgotten in a scene like this: women are in history and the text's attention to Ignoge shows how critical a juncture this is for Brutus's dynastic and nationalistic enterprise.

The transition to Brutus's line requires that Ignoge be a certain kind of female figure. As Gayle Rubin notes, "it would be in the interests of the smooth and continuous operation of such a [kinship] system if the woman in question did not have too many ideas of her own about whom she might want to sleep with. From the standpoint of the system, the preferred female sexuality would be one that responded to the desire of others, rather than one which actively desired and sought a response."[33] Because of her father's bargain, Ignoge must marry Brutus and go away from her homeland, but what if she could have refused? Such a refusal would have broken the dynastic enterprise just as surely as Brutus's actions did when he inadvertently killed both of his parents.

The text does not go so far as to allow Ignoge the choice of refusal; it only dramatizes her loss of lineage and her absorption into the narrow requirements of genealogy. While this affective moment may show patriarchal acknowledgement for the cost it renders from married women, Ignoge's only vocalization, her weeping, ends in silent sleep—her only subsequent mention in the text is at the opening of Book II, when Geoffrey relates that Brutus consummated his marriage with her and that "ex ea, genuit tres inclitos filios" (253) [by her, he had three famous sons]. Although her role in childbearing is preserved in that genealogical moment, a moment that in fact makes the rest of British history possible and makes her nearly-erased body its origin, the Greek princess has become a Trojan mother present only in the phrase "ex ea" embedded in her husband's genealogy.

Maintaining Lineage: Maternal Figures, Heirs, and the British Succession

Once the Brutus narrative has concluded, the *Historia regum Britanniae* takes on its most strictly genealogical form, listing the progression of kings and their heirs over the years, breaking this sequence to tell more detailed stories when the succession is at issue. The narrative's earlier concern for the creation of a Trojan ancestry becomes a preoccupation with maintaining this British lineage. As the royal line faces obstacles to producing each new generation, subordinate romance tales explore these crises by making women, whose presence is usually elided in strictly patrilineal genealogy, visible in the narrative. In Books II and III of the *Historia regum Britanniae*, female figures often complicate and re-negotiate the terms of primogeniture by asserting the interests of their own lineage; they also sometimes confirm the system and enable the narrative to return to the strict parataxis of the genealogy of kings. Spouses, such as the figures of Marcia and Genvissa, intercede between nations, negotiating between husbands and fathers. Maternal figures, such as Gwendolyn, Judon, and Tonvenna, assert the interests of their own lineage and act forcefully to decide conflicts between heirs, determining who should succeed to the throne and in what way. Cordelia, the daughter of Leir, also acts to protect her father's kingdom from usurpers and keep it for his own bloodline, by becoming a queen of Britain in her own right.

While the journey of a hero such as Brutus in a romance or quest narrative is one of struggle and reward, the journey of a female figure is often to passivity, to a narrative place where she can serve as the reward to the hero, ultimately gaining motherhood. This space, however, does have the potential for the activity of reproduction, and in this sense, female figures can claim the ambiguous "negative power of Demeter, the power to refuse, to withdraw, to plead and struggle anew, and undergo separation and loss."[34] A woman's "destiny" is to become the reward, to travel to the place where the man will find her; in the *Historia regum Britanniae*, however, women function not only as rewards and mothers. Because the story of each figure is situated within a genealogy and within the structure of succession, female figures act and react to that succession, questioning or partaking of the authority that space can give them. This final section will chart some of the kinds of actions these figures take to influence the way the text formulates the lineage of the kings of Britain. By presenting a range of often contradictory female positionings, the text not only explores tensions surrounding the politics of succession, but may also be presenting its various reading audiences with possibilities for women's behavior in politics.

Presented as one of the most illustrious and praiseworthy of women in early British history, Marcia literally holds a place in the succession of British kings. Her description paints her as an educated woman of accomplishment: she was "omnibus artibus erudita" (293) [skilled in all the arts], "consilio & sensu pollebat" (294) [extremely intelligent and most practical (101)] and "inter multa & inaudita quae proprio ingenio repererat invenit legem quam Brittones Marcianam appellaverunt" (293) [among the many extraordinary things for which she used her natural talent was a law she devised which was called the *Lex Martiana* (101)], which Geoffrey notes King Alfred translated into Old English as the Mercian Law. These qualities explain and authorize her most notable of accomplishments, becoming the monarch of England upon her husband's death, since the heir, her son Sisillius, was only seven. Although the *Historia regum Britanniae* says both she and her son hold power, Sisillius is not crowned until after her death. Marcia's status is ambiguous, but the *Historia regum Britanniae* harbors no reservations about her actions or her success. Upon the death of the king, the only other possible heir the text offers is a child, a critical situation which could easily have resulted in war and a contested succession. By allowing Marcia to stand in the succession as a praiseworthy and accomplished ruler, the genealogy is able to proceed without event to her son, Sisillius, to his son, Kinarius, to Danius, and to Morvidus before the line is ruptured anew.

Another queen of Britain, the Roman-born Genvissa, not only intervenes in the narrative to enable her son, Marius, eventually to succeed his father, but her very presence as the king's wife also enables British history to come through war with Roman forces led by her father, Claudius. In this situation, Britain almost certainly faces the end of its history as an independent monarchy, but through a marriage alliance offered by Rome, Britain will be preserved because the Roman emperor Claudius "preferebat ipsos sensu & sapientia subiugare quam dubium certamen inire...daturumque promittebat sese filiam suam si tantum modo regnum Britannie sub Romana postestate recognovisset" (323) [preferred to subdue them by plot and diplomacy rather than incur the hazard of a battle...promising to give him (Arvirargus, the British king) his own daughter, if only he would recognize that the kingdom of Britain was under Roman sway (121)]. The nobility tells Arvirargus, the current king, that "non esse ei dedecori subditum fuisse Romanis cum totius orbis inperio potirentur" (323) [it could be no disgrace for him to submit to the Romans, since they were the acknowledged overlords of all the world (121)]. This British submission to Rome is portrayed as canny diplomacy, with Arvirargus retaining authority over Britain and with the combined British and Roman forces subduing the Orkney Islands. This marriage plot allows British submission to be rehabilitated as an alliance. Genvissa is a traded women, as was Ignoge, but this exogamous pact becomes a strategy for colonization for the Romans and a face-saving surrender for the Britains.

Unlike Ignoge, however, who faded from the narrative after her marriage to Brutus, Genvissa's portrait and later intercession in the politics between the factions of her husband and her father illustrate how mature queens function in this part of the *Historia regum Britanniae*. Like most figures in this narrative, her initial description marks her as distinctive: not only is "tanta pulchritudo ut aspicientes in ammirationen duceret" (324) [her beauty such that everyone who saw her was filled with admiration] but also "ut maritali lege copulata fuit tanto fervore amoris succendit regem ita ut ipsam solam cunctis rebus preferret" (324) [once she had been united to him in lawful marriage, she inflamed the king with such burning passion that he preferred her company to anything else in the world (121)]. The *Historia regum Britanniae* paints Genvissa's beauty and the passion it inspires in her husband as the foundation of Arvirargus' success as a king, of his alliance with Rome, and of the prosperity of Britain itself. For Geoffrey of Monmouth, city-building and creating laws are the signs of the best of kings, and "as a result of" [unde] this marriage, Arvirargus and Claudius build the city of Kaerglou, or Gloucester, upon the site of the marriage ceremony, "in illo civitatem quae memoriam tatarum nuptiarum in futura tempora prebereta" (325) [a city which should perpetuate in times to come the memory of so happy a marriage (121)].

Genvissa's portrait so far has been economical, as are most in the *Historia regum Britanniae*. She serves not as the subject of a story, but as the kinship tie between two political factions and as the catalyst to her husband's actions. Her presence serves to create order, connection and conclusion in the continuing military narrative of Arvirargus's conflict with Rome. In the midst of another escalating political crisis, after British and Roman troops fight to a standstill, "facto mediante Genvissa Regina, concordes effecti sunt duces" (325) [Queen Genvissa acted as mediator and the two leaders made peace (122)]. Her last overt action in the narrative, Genvissa's mediation allows Arvirargus's reign to continue and prosper. Although her death goes unremarked, Arvirargus is eulogized by the *Historia* as one of the fiercest yet most beneficent of kings, and his descendants through Genvissa prosper for three generations until the last dies with no heir.[35] The figure of Genvissa enables the *Historia regum Britanniae* and the reign of Arvirargus to hold together through repeated political crises, and her line, bringing in the lineage of her father Claudius, becomes one of distinguished Romanized kings, Marius, Coilus, and Lucius. Like Marcia, the power that the figure of Genvissa exerts is uncodified by law and embodies contradictory perceptions of women—as a spouse and mother and daughter, she exerts influence and can cause actions to take place. Although her appearances are brief in this narrative of military actions and political strife between Britain and Rome, they pull these contentious strands together and allow the progress of history to continue. Like many female figures in the *Historia regum Britanniae*, Genvissa is nearly absent, yet her appearance is absolutely necessary.

Perhaps the most serious challenge to the establishment of the British royal lineage occurs in the very first generation after its founder Brutus. After Brutus's death, Britain is divided into thirds and distributed among his three sons with Albanaticus receiving Scotland, Kamber, Wales, and Locrinus, England. Locrinus quickly becomes the sole survivor, however, when Humber, a Hunnish invader, kills his two brothers. After vanquishing this threat, Locrinus alone rules Britain. This military conflict is dispatched in only a few lines in the *Historia regum Britanniae*, but the resulting difficulties in the politics of marriage for the newly established lineage of Britain create a long digression, illustrating ethnic and political tensions that must be resolved before the text can continue to the next generation.

Whom will Locrinus marry? In this, only the first generation after Brutus, who will be the mother of his heirs, the next rulers of Britain? The *Historia regum Britanniae* presents two candidates for the position, Gwendolyn, the daughter of the Trojan war hero, Corineus, one of Brutus's staunchest allies, and Estrildis, the daughter of a German king, taken from her father first by Humber and then seized by Locrinus as a battle prize. The portrayal of each of these women illustrates how pervasive the marriage alliance system was for twelfth-century culture, and how marri cession were mutually implicated.

The nar a context of the spoils of battle, as an ol that rewards whomever possesses her. ᵼ iil sibi retinens preter aurum & argentum ᵌtinuit quoque sibi tres puellas mire pul ᵗ nothing for himself except the gold and oard their ships. He also reserved for l n of striking beauty (76)]. Estrildis is si re that other men have coveted, for Hun erat] her when he was sacking Germany. .... is so extraordinary "quod non liviter reperiebatur quae ei conferri poterat Candorem carnis eius nec inclitum ebur nec nix recenter cadens nex lilia ulla vincebant" (254) [that it would be difficult to find a young woman worthy to be compared with her. No precious ivory, no recently fallen snow, no lilies even could surpass the whiteness of her skin (76)]. The descriptive terms used here are those of exotic material wealth in ivory and exquisite natural products in the snow and the lilies. The figure of Estrildis never escapes the status of an object to be taken or transported. Eventually Locrinus builds a special chamber for her under the city and keeps her as if a hidden treasure.[36]

Locrinus wishes to marry this German princess, but for the genealogical interests of this history, his desire represents a political crisis. The other claimant for the position of his wife, Gwendolyn, comes from Trojan lineage and her father, Corineus, controls Cornwall. Endogamous marriage seems to be set up as the safer course in this situation, and in the end, Gwendolyn's son does become king, continuing the Trojan-British line. But the two women and the interests they represent are presented in contradictory ways.

The political influence and rhetorical power of Gwendolyn's father, Corineus, are well illustrated in a long speech in which he forces Locrinus to marry his own Trojan daughter. As a hero of an earlier age and an advisor to Brutus, Corineus can expect continued status and reward for his past deeds through an alliance with Britain's current monarch. Instead, when Locrinus refuses to marry his daughter, he interjects: "haeccine rependis mihi Locrine ob tot vulnera quae in obsequio patris tui perpessus sum dum prelia cum ignotis gentibus committeret" (255) [these then, Locrinus, are the rewards you offer me in exchange for all the wounds which I have received through my allegiance to your father, at the time when he was waging war with unknown peoples? (76)]. This prospect of uniting with unknown people [ignotus gentibus] seems the final insult for Corineus, a man who led Trojan soldiers in vicious campaigns against the Franks in the Aquitaine, and who wrestled with the grotesque giant Gogmagog, gaining the isle of Britain for the Trojans. His speech continues, saying "ut filia mea postposita te conubio cuiusdam barbare summitteres?" (255) [my daughter is to be passed over and you are to demean yourself to the point where you will be prepared to marry some barbarian woman or other (76)]. Not only will Corineus lose status without a marriage alliance with the king, but by breaking his earlier betrothal to Gwendolyn, the king is embracing an alliance with those "ignotis gentibus," the non-Trojans with whom Corineus has spent his life fighting. Not only will Corineus be demeaned, but so will his king and the dynastic future of his people. In fact, Corineus, himself, begins the work of Locrinus' fall to barbarism, brandishing his ax and threatening to kill him, treating him as if he were one of the barbarian giants Corineus fought in his youth.

Locrinus' proposed marriage to Estrildis cannot survive such a political climate and, in fact, "amici utrorumque...Locrinum quod pepigerat exequi coegerunt" (255) [friends of each of them...forced Locrinus to carry out what he had promised (the marriage to Gwendolyn) (76)]. This enforcement of an endogamous marriage alliance, however, does not hold long—as soon as Corineus dies, Locrinus displaces Gwendolyn, making the German Estrildis his queen. But the interests enforced first by Corineus are taken up by his daughter. She fights to assert the rights of her own lineage, to make sure her own son, Madden, raised in Cornwall by her father Corineus, will inherit the throne rather than any children of the new queen, Estrildis. Gwendolyn becomes a military threat to Britain and to Locrinus when she returns to Cornwall, her father's seat of power, and gathering troops, harasses her husband's kingdom with border raids. The actions of Locrinus' wife prove fatal to him, for when their armies fight one another at the River Stour, "ubi Locrinus ictu sagitte percussus gaudia vitae amisit" (256) [Locrinus was struck by an arrow and so departed from the joys of this life (77)]. Geoffrey's narrative ominously observes that then "perempto igitur illo cepti Guend regni gubernaculum paterna insania furens" (256) [Gwendolyn took over the government of the kingdom, behaving in the same extravagant fashion as her father had done (77)]. While vicious militarism may have had its place in Brutus's best warrior, the text sees the same qualities in his daughter as characterizing a woman out of control.

The presence of two wives in the narrative with the accompanying possibilities for two branches to Brutus's and Locrinus's lineage create an ambiguous narrative and chaotic political situation. Gwendolyn receives no praise for enforcing her son's rights, perhaps because her campaign does kill the king. Once she leaves her military role, however, and takes on the role of mother, ruling Britain as caretaker for her son, Madden, she is completely rehabilitated. There are no stories told of her reign, only that "et cum tunc vidisset Maddan filium suum etate adultum sceptro regni insignivit illum contenta regione Cornubie dum reliquum vite dedeceret" (257) [as soon as she realized that her son Madden had grown to adulthood, she passed the sceptre of the realm to him, being content herself with the province of Cornwall for the rest of her life" (78). Although Gwendolyn did insure her son's succession, it was at the cost of the king's life. By the time her son takes the throne, however, she has become unthreatening to the progression of the narrative, which now proceeds with short and simple coordinate sentences. Madden, the son of Gwendolyn and Locrinus, proves a strong and unproblematic king.

Gwendolyn's assertion of the rights of her own lineage bring resolution to these marriage crises. Just as the value of her actions is ambiguous, the *Historia regum Britanniae* also refuses to condemn Locrinus for his repeated choice of a foreign princess. The fate of his concubine Estrildis and her daughter is even portrayed in poignant terms. Although they are both thrown into the Severn to drown, Gwendolyn proclaims that the river should henceforth bear the name of Habren [Sabrina] because she was the daughter of a king. Despite extinguishing a bloodline that could have continued to compete with that of her son, Gwendolyn provides an alternate heritage for Locrinus's other heir, marking the landscape with her name.

Two later female figures, Judon and Tonuvenna, intervene in the succession in equally dramatic fashion. The first, Judon, intercedes violently in the politics of succession. After six generations of smooth succession, two brothers, Ferrex and Porrex, fight about who should succeed their senile father. Theirs is the typical intrigue: Porrex tries to ambush Ferrex, who flees to France, returning with a Frankish army. In the ensuing battle, Ferrex is killed, leaving Porrex free to take the throne. The genealogical needs of the narrative seem to have been met—one son remains to rule Britain. But the text illustrates the dire consequences of this conflict by dramatizing the reaction of their mother, once news of Ferrex's death reaches her. Although both sons were equal in their claims to the throne, their Fury-like mother "commota in odium alterus versa est. Diligebat namque illum magis altero" [was consumed with hatred for Porrex for she had loved Ferrex more than him (88)]. Judon becomes a practically Ovidean figure when she "unde tanta ira ob mortem ipsius ignescebat ut...nacta ergo tempus quo ille sopitus fuerat aggrediture eum cum ancillis suis et in plurimas sectiones dilaceravit" [became so unbalanced by the anguish which the death of Ferrex has caused her that...she chose a time when Porrex was asleep, set upon him with her maid-servants and hacked him to pieces (88)]. The text portrays Judon as out-of-control in her need for vengeance,[37] but this murder does give her a decisive role in Britain's royal genealogy. More than just a silent mother who bears the next generation of princes, she decides which of the two heirs she prefers and forcefully acts to prevent the other from becoming king after the murder of her favorite. The text comments tersely on her actions, and shows how Judon has decisively destroyed the patriarchal narrative, by explaining that "exinde" [as a result of this] five kings of no name divided Britain and the people endured civil war for years to come. By including this mother's story, the *Historia regum Britanniae* exploits an opportunity to tell a sensational tale, but it also shows just how dangerous and threatening including a mother in a history can be.

While the intervention of Judon has succeeded in destroying the royal line, the *Historia regum Britanniae* immediately provides a counter-example of a mother whose intervention not only saves her husband's dynasty, but also by establishing peace between her two sons, makes Britain so powerful that its kings go on to conquer Rome itself. Tonuvenna is the mother of Belinus and Brennius, whose struggles over the succession dominate the early section of Geoffrey's history. After an alliance with the Danes and a battle on the high seas, Brennius finally invades his brother's British kingdom, leading a French army. At this battle, however, their mother, Tonuvenna, plays a crucial role that is diametrically opposed to the course that Judon took in the conflict between her sons. As the battle lines are drawn up, a dramatic scene unfolds, with Tonuvenna hurrying through the ranks, approaching Brennius with trembling steps, "estuabatque filium videre quem multo tempore non aspexerat" [passionately keen to see the son on whom she had not set eyes for so long (95)]. The text describes how mother's love drives her to hug and kiss him, and finally bare her breasts before him to make an impassioned plea for peace between her sons. Unlike Judon, whose passion for revenge has overturned the genealogical succession and cast Britain into chaos, when the *Historia* gives space to this mother, her passion serves narrative and national interests. Her excessive remonstrance is used to preserve the dynastic line.

In her speech itself, however, one of the few in direct speech accorded to a female figure, Tonuvenna elaborates a different concept of generational succession, one that emphasizes common family ties over the hierarchical interests of royal succession. She emphasizes the role her own body has played in creating this familial drama, exhorting Brennius to "memento fili memento uberum istorum quae suxisti matrisque tue uteri quo te opitex rerum in hominem ex non homine creavit unde te in mundum produxit angustiis mea viscera cruciantibus" [remember these breasts which you once sucked. Remember the womb of your mother, in which the creator of all things fashioned you as a man-child from stuff that was not yet human, bringing you forth into the world while the birth pangs tore at her vitals because of you (95–96)]. The invocation of her maternal body not only gives her the authority to compel Brennius to make peace with his brother, but it also gives them a shared origin as her sons, disrupting the hierarchy of inheritance and lineage. Although they both contest for their father's power, their mother changes their legacy to one of commonality and equality. Tonuvenna stresses this later in the speech when she argues that with one the King of the Allebroges and the other King of Britain, Brennius and Belinus are equals. Both brothers accept their mother's arguments and authority and make plans to invade Gaul together. In the genealogical schema, only one son can inherit his father's place, but through the intercession of Tonuvenna, two sons coexist in the narrative and bring Britain to unheard-of prominence by eventually conquering Rome itself. Including a mother in a pivotal space in his narrative has indeed re-affirmed the political needs of genealogy, but Tonuvenna has modified its operations to offer a creative transition of power from a father to both of his sons. Such maternal intervention allows Geoffrey of Monmouth to use his genealogical narrative in a new way. British history does not fall once again to its own vices, but rises to new prominence when two heirs fight on the same side, on equal terms, instead of against one another for the right to succeed their father.

Female figures in the powerful positions of wives and mothers intervene in the politics of succession to ensure the interest of their own lineage and offspring, often resolving problems for the progress of genealogy or proposing novel solutions, and sometimes compounding conflicts as in the case of Judon. In the story of Leir, however, there is no mother to intervene, and no son to reign. Leir must use marriage alliances to gain a suitable son-in-law to become his heir. Through Geoffrey's early telling of this subsequently well-known tale, Cordelia, however, becomes her father's heir, resolving his political problems and ruling Britain in her own right upon his death.

In this version of the tale, Leir attempts to continue his line and cope with his lack of a male heir by marrying his three daughters well and dividing Britain among them. In the midst of the folk motif of Leir questioning his daughters about the degree of their love for him and the theme of Leir's reversal of fortune, Leir shares the same dynastic concerns as earlier kings as "cogitavit regnum suum ipsis di-

videre easque talibus maritis copulare qui easdem cum regno haber-
ent" (262) [he made up his mind to divide his kingdom among them
(his three daughters) and to marry them to husbands whom he considered to be suited to them and capable of ruling the kingdom along
with them (81)]. These sons-in-law prove to be disloyal heirs when
they "insurexerunt in illum...abstulerunt autem ei regnum regiamque
potestatem quam usque ad illud tempus viriliter & gloriose tenuerat"
(265) [rebelled against him...took the remainder of his kingdom from
him and with it the royal power which up to then he had wielded
manfully and in all glory (83)]. Although Goneril and Regan fail to
care for their deposed father and his retinue, the political rupture be-
longs to Albany and Cornwall. These sons fail to provide a smooth
genealogical bridge from Leir's lineage to theirs, usurping rather than
succeeding to the throne.

Cordelia's marriage to the king of Gaul, however, provides an interesting counterpoint. Even though her father seeks to punish her by
marrying her off to a foreigner with no dowry but herself, her marriage provides a vital alliance that makes her Leir's true heir. The narrative, indeed, places her in the space of the prince seeking to restore
the proper line of her father's rule. The king of Gaul first marks her as
a genealogical bridge when he states that he wants to have children
with her ["ut heredes ex illa haberet" (265)]. But Cordelia's marriage
does not make her a mother; instead, with the riches of France at her
disposal, her marriage gives her the means to restore Leir to the British throne and ultimately reign as queen after his death and the death
of her husband. As Leir's heir, Cordelia continues his lineage in her
own right, not by linking a son-in-law to her father, or even providing
a grandson for whom she could be regent, and so is able to fully occupy the object space in her father's genealogy. As Geoffrey writes,
"Cordeilla ergo filia regni gubernacula adepta" (279) [Cordelia inherited the government of the kingdom of Britain (86)].

The narrative, however, does not allow Cordelia more than succession to the throne. She does not pass the kingship through her own
line since her two nephews, upon the deaths of their fathers Albany
and Cornwall, "indignati sunt" (270) [were angry] that Britain was
ruled by a woman. They raise armies against the queen and she meets
them in battle with her own forces until she is captured and impris-
oned. In prison, Geoffrey writes that "ob amissionem regni dolore ob-
ducta, sese interfecit" (271) [she grieved at the loss of her kingdom
and killed herself (87)]. Other women in the *Historia* rule Britain as

regents or are praised for their brilliance as queens. Cordelia's rule is never presented as illegitimate and she, indeed, had ruled peacefully for five years before her nephews' rebellion. So why are her nephews indignant at the queen's rule? Perhaps because if Cordelia were to pass the throne to her own heir, Leir's genealogy would become matrilineal and a direct threat to the patriarchy which stands behind most genealogical narrative. Cordelia can be the object, the heir, but not the subject of the next clause, providing an heir to the kingdom. When her nephews revolt, patriarchy re-asserts itself.

The story of the creation of Brutus as a new Trojan patriarch who will found the kingdom of Britain illustrates the *Historia regum Britanniae*'s concern with gender and genealogy. In Geoffrey of Monmouth's dual narrative form, female figures in romance tales also become situated structurally within genealogical history and questions of succession, and their tales can partake of the contradictory authority these positions may grant them. Some queens like Marcia and Genvissa stabilize the rule of their husbands, while other women intervene in the process by which their sons take power, such as Gwendolyn, Judon, or Tonuvenna. Cordelia, herself, holds the throne as her father's only worthy heir. When the two genres of history and romance meet, and the sequence of years is broken by the subordinate narration of an event, two social systems of economic and sexual regulation converge: the marriage practices of trading women through exogamy and endogamy and the succession practices of an emerging primogeniture. The generic tensions in the *Historia regum Britanniae* can thus be seen as a rhetorical response to the reproductive politics and power struggles of the early Plantagenet regime. The stories of Brutus and various female figures in the text could have offered audiences and subsequent authors positions from which to question or even alter the political and gender systems of which they were a part.

Patronage and reading practices are often difficult to determine for the various production contexts of the *Historia regum Britanniae* through the centuries. The next chapter will focus on a history in the tradition of Geoffrey, the Anglo-Norman chronicles of Nicholas Trevet, for which we can more soundly posit women's participation in the textual process, as well as find one important reader, Geoffrey Chaucer.

Women's Patronage and the Writing of History: Nicholas Trevet's *Les Cronicles* and Geoffrey Chaucer's *Man of Law's Tale*

icholas Trevet, a noted Dominican scholar of the early four-teenth century, used genealogy to situate female figures within his Anglo-Norman, universal history, *Les Cronicles*. Women become the origins for dynasties, intercessors in the succession process, and their marriages key political links. By using this strategy, Trevet may have been responding to the influence of a woman patron, Mary of Woodstock, a daughter of Edward I and sister to Edward II. Mary may even have been involved in the composition process. The centerpiece of *Les Cronicles*, an entry commonly known as the "Tale of Constance," establishes its heroine as a key genealogical link, with her travels and adventures explaining a gap in the succession of Roman emperors. When Geoffrey Chaucer rewrites this entry as a hagiographic romance for his *Man of Law's Tale*, he leaves the historiographic context and content of the "Tale of Constance" behind. By changing the genre of Constance's story, he emphasizes her humility and passivity and so undermines the earlier chronicle's complex vision of the roles women could play in dynastic politics.

As a "universal chronicle," in fact the first of this genre in Anglo-Norman, *Les Cronicles* summarizes the events of the Christian world from the Creation through Biblical and ancient history.[1] It includes the legendary, early history of Britain and France, as well as accounts of more recent kings. Writers of universal histories compiled them from earlier histories and structured their vast material through references to events earlier in the chronicle and to subsequent sections. Trevet, however, particularly used genealogical narratives to create links not only among sections of text, but also across the times, geographical spaces, and political entities he covers.

Trevet's text also includes female figures in his genealogical narratives at key junctures between cultures. He portrays the Nativity as the birth of an heir firmly in the human lineage of St. Anne. He foregrounds the Empress Matilda as the founder of the Plantagenet line in England, and he includes his patron, her female relations and their offspring, in long family lists. Women from ancient and Biblical history, the "mothers of us all," as one of Trevet's anecdotes puts it, intervene in the dynastic politics of their day. Most notably, the "Tale of Constance," is the longest entry of the chronicle, occupying nearly the physical center of the text. In this central piece, surrounded by genealogical lists, and further demarcated by a change in the introductory formula for each entry from before the tale to after it, Trevet excavates his heroine's story in order to explain a seeming gap in the succession of Rome. In the process, he creates a figure who forms her own identity and takes her place within her family's lineage.

Scholars have long noted that Trevet probably shaped the chronicle to please his patron, but more recent scholarship on women patrons in the Middle Ages, as well as records of Trevet's relationship with patrons of others of his works, suggests that Mary could have been involved in both the selection of material and the making of stylistic decisions. If we consider the possibility of Mary of Woodstock's active involvement with Trevet's composition of the text, in a kind of collaborative authorship,[2] we cast a new perspective on this material: how and why was it selected and how was it composed? Scholars of medieval women's history have recently shown that through their control over the patronage process, aristocratic women were not only able to aid their families' attempts to legitimize their current power by valorizing their own history, but these women patrons were also able to insure the insertion of themselves and their female ancestors into public displays of their lineage.

Both the content and rhetorical structure, as well as the circumstances of the production of *Les Cronicles*, can lead us to imagine that Mary sought such an end for her chronicle. As popular texts, chronicles were read publicly as court entertainment. Trevet announces the purpose of *Les Cronicles* to be to provide a source for basic historical information for a popular audience and it appears to have served this purpose. Fourteen copies survive from the period, with a late four-teenth-century copy found in the library of Thomas of Woodstock, a member of the royal family. At the end of the century, Chaucer still used Les Cronicles as his main source for basic historical knowledge.[3]

By examining not only the content and structure of the compendium of stories from the past, but also the politics and economics of the patronage system that produced it, we find that gender participates in both these aspects of the textual process. The stories of women enmeshed in this narrative could have provided positions from which medieval women and men could affirm or question contemporary gender roles. In the chronicle produced by the collaboration of Nicholas Trevet and Mary of Woodstock, the power to represent the past and legitimate the politics of the present could also explore how medieval women could act in an age where family and national politics were the same arena. When Chaucer's later version markedly reduces the figure of Constance by taking her out of the context of genealogical history, producing a humble and suffering woman, drifting through European seas in her rudderless boat, that arena has perhaps changed, with the options for women to influence literary production fewer than in Mary's day earlier in the century.

Les Cronicles and Women's Patronage

The dynamics of the Plantagenet court culture in which Trevet participated were driven by the royal family's recurring need to legitimate and publicize its power. By producing romances that glorified court culture and historical texts that retold their own family legends and genealogies, the Plantagenets were able to create and disseminate myths of their own rule.[4] The production of texts in this courtly climate depended upon the dynamics of patronage—nobles needed knowledgeable clerics to compile and create these tales, and writers like Trevet[5] could not produce narratives without an awareness of courtly politics or how the texts they produced would be used at court.

While scholars have long recognized that both women and men functioned as patrons of literature in medieval courts, most perceptions of women patrons have seen their interests as limited to the production of romances and religious texts. It is a commonplace that Eleanor of Aquitaine promoted courtly literature and that her grand-daughter Marie de Champaigne subsidized the writings of Chretien de

Troyes. But perhaps because historiography, especially Latin history, has been primarily considered a genre produced for the education and socialization of boys who would be kings and military leaders,[6] the importance that female patronage held for the production of history is only beginning to be recognized. Through subsidizing public displays of lineage in the forms of architecture and texts, requisitioning texts for the education of their children, as well as vernacular translations for court use, and by establishing networks of women patrons across the generations of their families, aristocratic medieval women produced histories for the same political, dynastic and educational purposes as did patrons who were men.

Patronage was a familial expectation for the Plantagenets, but so was promoting the family and their lineage.[7] In fact, because they could capitalize on women's traditional roles as the caretakers of the dead, aristocratic women were well-positioned to promote an awareness of the past through patronage activity that would popularize the lives and deeds of the family's ancestors. For instance, as patron of the Abbey of Fontevrault, Eleanor of Aquitaine not only educated her children there and retired within its walls, but she also established a necropolis for her family at the abbey. This practice was taken up by her daughters when their marriages took them into other royal houses. Miriam Shadis calls this practice "a way to perpetuate their own personal influence indefinitely, gaining power for themselves as well as their families" which would "remind all who saw them—especially future members of their family—of the elements of their lineage and family structure, and power."[8] By their supervision of the design and iconography of such burial monuments, politically astute Plantagenet queens kept their family's lineage, and their own place within it, before the public eye.

In this same capacity as a caretaker of the dead, an aristocratic woman could foster the writing of histories that would portray ancestors and their deeds in a heroic fashion and would keep the present family members' connections to a venerable past in active play in contemporary politics. For instance, Yolande, the countess of Saint-Pol, sponsored the first vernacular translation of the Latin history known as the *Pseudo-Turpin*. The production of the *Pseudo-Turpin* in northern France was part of a complex response on the part of local nobles to the increasing threat posed by the Capetian king Philip Augustus to their sovereignty and their perceived loss of status to the rising burghers of Flanders. By creating and re-creating a past where ancestors hold strong moral and political ground, Yolande's sponsorship of the *Pseudo-Turpin* not only soothed her people's social anxieties, but sought to shore up their faltering political fortunes.[9]

In the same way, Eleanor of Castile, the wife of Edward I of England and the mother of Mary of Woodstock, promoted her own family history and consolidated her political authority in her ancestral lands of Ponthieu. Soon after she became Countess of Ponthieu in 1279, Eleanor commissioned a romance about her reputed ancestor, Isembart. Given her upbringing in the Castellian court where historiography flourished and her introduction to the Anglo-Norman ancestor cults in her husband's circles, Eleanor's "ability to integrate such influences in or through the written word had led her to cultivate 'Count Isembart' as an ancestor and a type for the counts of Ponthieu with an eye toward legitimizing a political agenda for her new inheritance."[10] In these examples of Yolande and Eleanor, we find more of a tradition for women's strategic patronage of historiography than has previously been acknowledged.

The political advantage of promoting ancestors and lineage, however, was only one reason women were involved in the production of historical narratives. Women were educators as well, and in this capacity they ordered specific texts for their children, as well as vernacular translations of important Latin texts for the court. For many, patronage that improved the literary and cultural life of the court was a familial expectation. Royal women supervised the early education of boys and the entire education of their daughters, and they clearly considered a knowledge of world and family history essential to their children before they entered the adult courtly world themselves. When mothers ordered primers, psalters, and histories for their children, they prescribed specific contents to the writer or scribe, and so exerted a strong influence on their intellectual, social and ideological development."[11]

In the Plantagenet court, historiography also played a role in women's education, helping foreign brides newly arrived in the family to learn about their new kingdom and lineage. When Eleanor of Castile first arrived in England, she received a copy of Matthew Paris's life of Edward the Confessor, and in 1290, a vernacular chronicle was produced to teach Eleanor's daughter the history and language of Brabant, where she would marry the duke's son.[12] Learning history and language through this kind of historiography could help a young woman bridge the gap between the culture of the court in which she grew up and the court into which she married.

In so providing for their daughters' education, royal women not only helped them acclimate to a new culture, but also helped to create, over the years, networks of women actively engaged in this kind of patronage. Eleanor of Aquitaine may be the best known of medieval women patrons, but her legacy was continued and spread through Europe as her daughters and granddaughters continued her tradition of literary patronage in the courts into which they married. They can be credited, for instance, with spreading the manuscripts of Geoffrey of Monmouth's *Historia regum Britanniae*.[13] One of Eleanor of Aquitaine's descendants, Eleanor of Castile, wife of Edward I, brought women's patronage back to the English court when she established her own scriptorium. The records of her "wardrobes," or personal entourage, show that she employed several scribes who traveled with her and that they purchased "vellum, ink, quills, pigments, gold leaf, and mucilage—all 'for the queen's books.'" The maintenance of this scriptorium shows not only Eleanor's interest in literary culture and production, but as John Carmi Parsons argues, because a personal scriptorium freed her from dependance on independent artisans, illustrates that the queen valued having complete control and supervision over the production of manuscripts.[14] Upon her death, Edward I pensioned her scribes and disbanded the scriptorium, with her daughters inheriting her books.

This practice was the usual one: daughters inherited their mothers' books as part of the personal and household effects that were traditionally inherited matrilineally.[15] More than simply books, however, were often passed on from mother to daughter. Karen K. Jambeck argues that particularly in England, literary patronage was a practice by which women defined themselves and their social roles, and that this practice was passed on cognatically. Mothers and daughters, as well as grandmothers, sisters, aunts, nieces, and cousins, formed female networks of patrons, who learned and reinforced practicing patronage and producing texts among themselves.[16]

This, then, was the sort of court within which Nicholas Trevet wrote his Anglo-Norman chronicle. Eleanor of Castile had certainly exerted a strong influence upon the production of texts on top of the usual Plantagenet habit of patronage and their preference for ancestral history. Eleanor, herself, founded the London priory of Dominicans[17] which Trevet headed in the years in which he wrote *Les Cronicles.* The five daughters of Eleanor of Castile, Mary of Woodstock among them, could have participated in this kind of women's culture of patronage.

Mary of Woodstock (1279–1332?), the fourth daughter of Edward I and Eleanor of Castile, entered the convent of Amesbury at about the age of seven (1285) as one of several companions to her grandmother, Eleanor of Provance, upon her retirement there. Her adult life, however, was not a completely cloistered one. As the daughter of the king, she played a role at court, often meeting state visitors and acting as a companion to the queen (Edward I's second wife) in 1305. Her father and later her brother, Edward II, supported her financially and she spent her time traveling among the family's and her own properties and on pilgrimages, raising greyhounds, and even gambling. Mary was a nun, however, and as such was the "visitor" of her order for England. Since Amesbury was a cell of the Abbey at Fontevrault, Mary was effectively the deputy in England of the Abbess of Fontevrault. Mary occupied an important place in both the secular and religious worlds of late thirteenth-early fourteenth century England.

Within both these worlds, Mary had ample precedent for the practice of literary patronage. Her mother, Eleanor of Castile, not only thrived on patronage but used it to educate her daughters, for they were "well-educated and of a literary turn—friars of her favored Dominican order lived with her children and probably taught them."[18] At Amesbury, Mary could have received further indoctrination, for Mary's grandmother, Eleanor of Provance, with whom she entered the convent, actively sponsored art and literature. Mary of Woodstock stood in the midst of a network of female patronage.

Given the precedents set by her female relations, Mary could have been a patron involved in the production and selection of material for Nicholas Trevet's *Les Cronicles.* Trevet dedicated the text to her, and the four earliest of the nine extant, fourteenth-century, Anglo-Norman manuscripts include the dedicatory rubric: "Ci comencent les cronicles qe frere Nichol Trevet escrit a ma dame Marie la fillie mon seignur le roi d'Engleterre, le fitz Henri" (Rutherford v. 2.1).[19] The early date of this rubric shows that the text during its writing was intended for Mary.[20] *Les Cronicles* includes much Plantagenet family lore that cannot be found in other sources. This fact, coupled with the dedication, leads Parsons to conclude that Mary definitely requested this chronicle and that Trevet as "Prior of the London Dominicans and an internationally renowned scholar, had no need to court Mary's patronage with an unsolicited work."[21] Earlier scholars have concluded that with such a patron, Trevet must have crafted the text to please her.[22] A collaborative relationship, however, could also have been the case—especially since the dedicatory letter of Trevet's second Latin history indicates that he worked closely with the patron of that work, Hugh, Archdeacon of Canterbury, and incorporated his suggestions. Trevet relates that he presented Hugh with an early version of the *Historia*, but upon his patron's urging, added more to the account, especially much Roman history from Livy. Trevet felt indebted to this patron and "wished to please him" with the material.[23] The dedicatory letter reveals that Trevet's historical interests, for he had previously written a commentary on Livy, meshed with those of this patron and that Trevet adapted his text to suit them both.

Les Cronicles was well-received[24] and successful in the years after Mary's death (c. 1332), gaining a broad audience. Trevet continued to work on the text after his patron's death and episodes such as the conflict between Louis of Bavaria and John XXII imply that there existed a French reading audience interested in matters of sovereignty. The manuscript history also shows that *Les Cronicles* was copied at many different places, implying that different kinds of readers had commissioned this history for their use. The chronicle was well-received, since early editions were produced in quick succession,[25] and this popularity continued through the fourteenth century, when Legge explains it became widely known and quoted. Nine Anglo-Norman manuscripts remain from the fourteenth century, as well as two later copies.[26] In 1397, two copies of *Les Cronicles* were listed in the library of Thomas of Woodstock, Earl of Gloucester, great-nephew of Mary and brother of John of Gaunt. Robert Pratt concludes: "*Les Cronicles* was clearly a history well known to the family of Edward III." Pratt also makes a compelling argument that Geoffrey Chaucer was among later readers of Trevet's complete history and used themes and echoes from the chronicle throughout his corpus, not simply in his adaptation of the "Tale of Constance." He and Robert Correale claim that Chaucer, especially given his preference for French over Latin, used Trevet's history for much of his general historical knowledge.[27] In about 1400, when Anglo-Norman was fading as a literary language of the aristocracy, *Les Cronicles* was translated into Middle English.

Given these tantalizing clues into not only how patronage functioned among the Plantagenet women, but also Trevet's working relationship with another dedicatee, *Les Cronicles* may have been written
both for Mary of Woodstock and according to her wishes. Trevet and
Mary could have worked together in a kind of collaborative authorship to produce this history. By participating in a textual project that
appealed to both of their historical interests, and which had a lasting
impact in fourteenth-century England, Mary could be both patron and
politician within her courtly and familial circles.

Genealogy, Women, and Dynastic Politics

The text of *Les Cronicles* itself offers tantalizing suggestions that
Trevet did indeed write gender in a way that would have appealed to
his women readers and suited the political needs of his patron. Trevet's chronicle tells stories that foreground women as integral parts of
genealogy and enact their participation and intervention in the politics of succession as normative behavior. In other texts produced under the auspices of female religious, gender becomes foregrounded and
contested. For instance, in her recent analyses of the iconography of
St. Anne and the Holy Family, Pamela Sheingorn finds that gender
and genealogy are contested sites, with St. Anne and her families often supplanting the figure of the "Tree of Jesse." She writes that the
"possible association between female patronage and the prominent
inclusion of Christ's family through the female line hints at a deliber-
ate focus on matriliny among female religious."[28] Joan Ferrante, in her
examination of several Latin histories that were written by men for
female patrons, also concludes that "histories written for women give
more attention to women in history, naming queens as well as kings,
mothers as well as fathers since a mother's illustrious genealogy can
be a major claim to her son's legitimacy in a disputed succession.
They record alliances by marriage as well as wars and they tell the
stories of women of note, biblical, ancient, and modern."[29] Because
medieval histories were often written to give readers models of proper
behavior, foregrounding female figures in history suited the tastes of
women readers who held power in the present.[30]

Les Cronicles is an encyclopedic history. Its first half compiles
events from the Old Testament, with the early, often mythic histories
of Persia, Egypt, Syria, Rome, and Greece, and the legendary history of
early Britain, from Geoffrey of Monmouth, interspersed within. After
the birth of Christ, Trevet recounts the early history of the Christian

church and its popes, along with a more historical version of Saxon England and the Franks. In its second half, *Les Cronicles* becomes a narrower history of the kings of England after the conquest, but it never completely loses its universal scope, returning consistently to news of the activities of various popes and saints.[31]

In its organization, *Les Cronicles* shares another mark of the universal chronicle. Unlike annals such as the *Anglo-Saxon Chronicles*, universal histories tend to give some order and pattern to their material by frequently making reference to material supplied in previous, as well as subsequent sections of the text. In Trevet's text these references emphasize the place of Britain in the European and Christian world by stressing narratives of genealogy and intermarriage as important ways that British history forges links with this larger world history. Narrating genealogy and intermarriage serves to structure and link broad sections of text.

Even aside from the "Tale of Constance," to be treated in the final section of this chapter, the text acknowledges and sanctions female power in stories as disparate as the Persian king Darius's test for his court, Old Testament accounts that feature the dynastic intervention of Judith, Rebecca, and the daughters of Lot, and Nero's demand that his advisors enable him to conceive a child. The Virgin Mary and her maternal relatives are situated as the origin of the Christian line, and the Empress Matilda features prominently as the source of the Plantagenet line in England. Mary of Woodstock and her immediate female relations are also featured in this lineage. While these portrayals of female figures can be problematic in medieval texts, the inclusion of women in stories and reiterations of genealogies in *Les Cronicles* creates models of powerful women acting within history for the consumption of courtly readers.

Trevet crystallizes the active political roles women could hold in history and the genealogical importance of reproduction by relating a short parable from the court of the Persian king, Darius. In a way, the portrayal of women in *Les Cronicles* follows these two formulae of the parable of Darius, that women can intervene with male power and that they give birth to all. When the king offers a treasure to the courtier who can tell him what is the strongest thing on earth, many suggest "vin" or "roi en son real power" (2.77.5–6) ["wyne" or "hys royall power" (80)]. But the winning answer is offered by the man who advises Darius that "femme et verite passent totes choses en force"

qare countre verite ne put nule chose rester.../.Et nii ad si fort ne si
cruel prince ne roi, qe femme ne adaunte. Et rois et emperours sount
neez de femmes" (2.77.6–10) ["woman and trouthe passeth all thyng
in strenght, for ageynst trouthe may nothyng resyste ner wyth-
stonde.... And there ys none so strenge ner so cruel a prince neyther
kyng but a woman may apese hys crewelte. And all kynges and other
persones be bore of women" (80)]. This parable acknowledges
women's central role in the political arena. Although they do not hold
power in the traditional political sense, they may influence it and this
is all to the good. Although they cannot be kings, they give birth to
kings, thereby further participating in the politics of succession.

Women take active roles in determining questions of succession
and national destiny in the Biblical stories of Judith, Rebecca, and
Lot's daughters. Trevet presents their actions as necessary to further
the progress of divine and dynastic history. In the familiar story of
Judith and Holofernes, told in only thirty lines directly preceding the
incident at the court of Darius, Judith's heroic interventions save the
ethnic and religious identity of her people. Holofernes's invasion is
set up as a crisis of faith for the Jews: their temple is destroyed and
they have been forced to worship a foreign king as a god. Judith appears immediately on the scene—"la tres noble vidve jevuess Judith
de le linage Ruben, Trop seint et bele dame bien et deliciousement
aourne" (2.76.9–10) ["the Iewesse Iudythof the lynage of Ruben a full
holy wydow and a full fair lady wele deliciously and fresshely ar-
rayed" (79)] and within three sentences she has captured the desire of
Holofernes, cut off his head, and returned to the Hebrew city of Be-
thuly. This part of the narrative receives the most emphasis for "et
tut le people de la cite vient joiousement countre lui" (2.76.20) ["all
the people of the cyte come full ioyfully metyn her" (79)]. She reveals
the head of the enemy while her people rejoice and dedicates his ar-
mor and head to God. These events are so striking that one of
Holofernes's own men "guerpi la ley de paens, et fu circumcis, et se
joint al poeple de Judeus et lour ley" (2.76.22–24) ["forsoke the law of
paynemes and was circumcised and joined himself to the people of
Jewes and to their law" (79)]. At a moment of great crisis for the Jewish nation, Judith's intervention is recognized by them as a pivotal
and transforming act, enabling them to retain their religious and racial identity against non-believing invaders. As the entry draws to its
close, Trevet tells us conventionally that Judith dies at the age of 105

and is buried with her husband. Judith's actions do not threaten the narrative of history, but enable it to progress.

Likewise when Rebecca intervenes in inheritance, her actions are presented as part of a sequence of events that do not subvert the will of Isaac, but instead fulfill the prophecy of God. Her intervention is necessary to the future of Jewish and Christian history. From the beginning, the struggle between Esau and Jacob, even within their mother's womb, is one between their rights of succession and the status of their subsequent lineages, for "et qant Rebecca fu enceinte de vifs enfauntz, les enfantz hurtlerent ensemble en le ventre lour mere. Dont ele ala de conseiller Dieux qoi ce devoit amounter, qi li respondi qe de les deus fitz, q'ele avoit en son ventre, vendroient deus manere de gentz, et qe l'eisne frere ove son linage serviroit le puisne" (2.16.27–17.2) ["when Rebecca was grete and quycke of II chyldre, the chyldre hurteled to geder in her [their] moder wombe. Wherefore she went and prayed of the counseyle of God what that shuld amounte and mene whyche answered to her. Tharof the II sonnes that she had in her body, shal come II maner of peple, and that the elder brohter with his lynage shall serve the younger" (16)].

The account of Isaac's blessing following this prophecy is much reduced from the Old Testament version but preserves the details that show it to be fulfilling God's prophecy. Trevet makes no mention of Isaac's favoring Esau because he brought him meat from his hunt (Genesis 25.28), but says instead that once Isaac was blind, he unwittingly "forclost Esau, son fitz eisne, de sa benisoun de eisnesce par non sa chance, et dona la benisoun a Jacob par la queintise. et la doctrine sa femme Rebecca, qi ama plus Jacob" (2.17.11–15) ["forclosed Esau hys Elder sonne of his blessyng of Eignest (elder right)...and gave the blessing to Jacob by the acueyntaunce and the techyng of hys wyfe Rebecca which loved more Jacob" (16)]. Rebecca's responsibility is preserved in this account, but she is not shown purposely coaching Jacob to supplant his brother as in the Old Testament account. Trevet's chronicle, like the Biblical text, quickly explains Esau's own responsibility for his loss by telling how on another occasion, he had traded his birthright to his younger brother for a porridge. In Trevet's account, Rebecca's intervention not only helps make her son Jacob the heir to his father, Isaac, but once he attains this status, the text can go forward to tell how Jacob becomes the father of the twelve tribes of Israel. His mother's sanctioned role in fulfilling God's prophecy enables him to become the new patriarch whose lineage and history this text will recreate.

In the account of Lot's daughters, Trevet also refrains from any diatribes against their incest and, in fact, seems almost to justify their actions, given the paramount importance of lineage and reproduction, as reasonable. Trevet simply notes that the daughters of Lot are not mentioned in the book of Genesis because of "la mervellouse deceite" (2.14.18) ["mervelous deceit" (14)] they performed against their father.[32] He, however, goes on to restore the story he claims is omitted by Genesis and to list two reasons for their actions: first, that their mother had been turned into a pillar of salt and second, that "q'elles savoient qe ja n'i avoit espoir de multiplier lour linage par engendrure de lour mere, qe ja fuit tourne en autre estrange nature, pur ce, pur doute q'eles avoient qe lour linage et nature de homme devoit failler, cestes deus filles Loth enyvererent lour piere de fort vyn" (2.14.29–15.3) ["they know that never was hope or trust to multiply their lineage by any engendrure of her mother whyche then was turnyed into another straunge nature. Ffor that and for dought that they had that theyre lynage and kynde of man shulde fayle, these ii doughteres mad her ffader loth dronkyn of stronge wyne..." (14)]. The incestuous actions of Lot's daughters are cast as a perhaps legitimate concern about their future lineage under the extraordinary circumstance of their mother's transformation. They receive no censure and Trevet simply turns to a section about Abraham once he explains that Lot was so intoxicated that he did not recognize his daughters.

The parable of Darius argues that not only do women intervene in politics, but that they gain power by being mothers. Reproduction is thereby characterized by Trevet as an exclusively female source of power and status when he includes and condemns the bizarre story of Nero's desire to give birth. After first killing his own mother so that he may look into her womb and find the place of his own origins, even after "les sages clercs le repernoient et disoient qe lei de nature denie qe fitz occie sa mere, pur ce qe ove grantz travauset dolours enfante" (2.130.4–7) ["the wyse clerkes repreuved hym and seyde that the lawe of Nature deyeth and is contrary to all reason that the son should slee hys moder, and specially for many grete travayles and dyseases that she suffereth in hys byrthe" (138)], Nero decides to inquire further into the act of childbirth by demanding that his advisors find a way for him to experience pregnancy. They answer that this is impossible because it is "encontre nature" (2.130.10) ["against kind"].

Once Nero threatens them with death, however, the philosophers "lui donerent un pocion, et firent q'une reine nesceoit en son ventre. Et puis son ventre comencea a emfler, issint q'il entendi q'il estoit gros de un enfant. Et quant il ne poeit plus lunge suffrir les dolours qe la reine lui fesoit en son ventre, dist as philosphers: 'Hastes tost le temps d'enfantier' et cil lui donerent une pocion, et li firent vomir la reine qe trop estoit hidouse a regarder" (2.130.11–18) ["gafe to hym a drynk, and made that a frog was consyved in hys body. And than afterwarde ys wreched bely began to swelle in somoche that he undresotde that he was grete wyth chylde. And whan he myght not lenger suffre the dyseases and peynes that the frog had wrought in his cursed body, he sayde agayn to the philosophers, 'haste ye nowe and hye ye fast, that I may bere my chylde orelles ye shall dye.' And then there the philosophers gafe to hym a nother drynke and made hym to cast oute the frog be vomyte chyche was hydows and howge for to loke opon" (139)]. Nero's goal of "motherhood," "esprover dolour des femme" (2.130.2) [preue the disease and travayle of wemen" (139)], has been achieved, but only in a grotesque parody of childbirth. The text condemns his actions because they degrade and minimize the pain and travail of mothers in childbirth.

Nonetheless, Nero tries to legitimate his perverse desires and unnatural child by ordering the frog to be well fed and raised up in a stone enclosure built for it. But when the people of Rome finally drive their emperor out of the city to his own, self-inflicted death, they do not forget his "offspring": "puis les Romeins engetterent de la cite la reine qe estoit en la vousteure enclose, et la lapiderent" (2.130–29–30) ["the Romans caste oute of the Cytee that frog the whych was there kept enclosyd. And there they stonyd that frog to dethe" (139)]. Although only one item on a long list of Nero's outrageous behaviors, the birth and death of Nero's frog-child illustrates that interloping into actual generation is not only against "nature" or "kind," but that the people of Rome will act decisively and publicly to put an end to this small, yet threateningly unnatural scion of Nero—his amphibian lineage will be stoned and destroyed. By condemning Nero for degrading birth, the text puts motherhood forward as something to be valued and its attendant travail and pain as warranting respect.

Trevet's version of the Nativity is presented as a story of the birth of an heir, foregrounding Christ's mother Mary who gives him his human lineage through the matrilineal ancestry and progeny of his grandmother St. Anne. Trevet's version of the nativity shows that Mary and Anne's acts of reproduction are ones that cannot be glossed over in the genealogy because their bodies provide the human mate- rial for the divine child. The birth of Jesus begins a new book in the chronicle and Trevet quickly relates the familiar events of the birth in Bethlehem, the visit of the three kings, the circumcision, and the flight into Egypt. Trevet is at pains to describe how this divine birth fits into human history and so explains at length the Christ child's genealogical ties to human families. His mother and female relations achieve great prominence in this moment, for following this brief ac- count is a section three times its length in which Trevet explains that Jesus received his name because Joseph was of the line of Judah. After briefly listing eight generations of ancestors for Joseph, the chronicle turns to Jesus's mother, Mary, to explain in the French text, but in capitalized titles in the Middle English "ore dirroms del linage Nostre dame Seinte Marie del part son piere" (2.113.25–26) ["NOWE WE MUST SEY OF THE LINAGE OF OURE LADY SEYNT MARY OF HER FADER SIDE" (119)]. After listing the generations from David to Mary, the French text describes similarly, with another heading in the Middle English, "ore dirroms del linage Nostre Dame Seinte Marie de la part sa miere" (2.114.4–5) ["NOWE HERE FOLOWETH THE LY- NAGE OF OURE LADY ON HER MODER SYDE" (120)]. This sec- tion interestingly focuses not on the ancestors of Saint Anne, but instead after explaining who her father was and that Mary the mother of Jesus was born of Anne's first marriage with Ioachim, the text lists two other marriages for Anne and the children she bore. This genera- tion, in its turn, gave birth to children who become Biblical heavy- weights: Joseph, Judas, Thaddeus, Simon, James the lesser from Anne's second marriage and "Johan l'evangelistre et James le Maior" (2.114.16) ["Saint John the noble evangelist and James the Apostle" (120)] from the third marriage. And finally, the text explains the line- age of John the Baptist, born to Elizabeth, the daughter of St. Anne's sister.

As Pamela Sheingorn observes, many medieval treatments of the birth of Christ used genealogies such as the Tree of Jesse to eclipse Mary's maternal role. Sheingorn emphasizes that the prominence of the Tree of Jesse attests to more than simply a shift to genealogical perceptions, for

> Christ's genealogy was deliberately being seen in terms of patriarchy.
> Choices were made that deemphasized the basic truth that, in order for

Christ to have a divine father, his other, human parent had to be a woman. Apparently unwilling to give full recognition to the fact that a female link had been forged into the patriarchal chain at an especially crucial point, most makers of such images in the thirteenth and fourteenth centuries chose instead to trace the lineage of Christ from the male founder, Jesse, through a male line of patriarchs and kings to the male child, Christ.

Given this context, Sheingorn concludes that depictions of Christ's lineage through St. Anne and the Holy Family, much like the one we have found in Trevet's account of the nativity, can be read as "conscious rebuttals of the patriarchal Tree of Jesse." Christ may be a god made man, but his bodily self comes to him from the feminine, his mother and her female relations. In the midst of his history, Trevet foregrounds matriliny to include and celebrate Mary's role in the most key moment of human history.[33]

Plantagenet historiography focused very much on creating origins such as Troy or King Arthur to legitimate their rule. Trevet's description of the descent of the Plantagenet family also looks back to an origin, a matrilineal one in the person of the Empress Matilda, the mother of their founder Henry II, who fought against Stephen over her father's throne. Trevet addresses the complexity of the succession by not only emphasizing how Matilda provides Henry II with his claim to the English throne, from her father, Henry I, but also how in Trevet's eyes, she also gives him a Saxon lineage. It takes Trevet several pages to explain how the descendants of the sons of Edmund Ironsides, sent to Hungary under the reign of the Danish king Knut, manage to become connected to the Scottish royal line, and to provide a bride to William the Conqueror, an ancestor of Matilda, Henry II's mother, thereby giving Henry Saxon blood. Trevet can then proclaim "et issint faillent les Normaundz regner en Engleterre par touz jours, et le tres noble sanc regal des Sessons en le rengne d'Engleterre restore de part la miere cist Henri, roi d'Engleterre" (2.306.28–307.1) ["thus failed the Normans to reign in England for all way. And the full noble blood of Saxons in the realm of England restored on the mother's side of this king Henry of England" (332)]. Henry II is called "Henry, the Empress's son" in a later, fourteenth-century chronicle, the prose *Brut*, and this emphasis on his maternal lineage surfaces in Trevet's history.[34] In Trevet's recounting, Matilda's claim and through her, Henry II's, provides the one of the sources for the legitimacy and origins of the Plantagenet family line.

Through the generations of Plantagenets, Trevet includes his patron's female relatives, describing whom they marry and what children are born to them, including Mary and her own four sisters. In fact, some of the Anglo-Norman manuscripts include diagrams of the family of Edward II.[35] Although not presented as a matrilineal pattern of descent, including so many female connections creates broad sections of cognatic kinship within the larger agnatic succession. As David Herlihy defines these types of lineage, agnatic lineage "becomes a kind of fellowship of males, stretching backwards and forwards over time. Women no longer serve as the nodules through which pass the surest kinship ties. The daughter is treated as a marginal member of her father's lineage and after her marriage, her children will leave it entirely." The cognatic system, as opposed to the agnatic, is "ego-focused," that is, focused on the first-person, nominative position (Latin *ego*) as the starting point for determining lineage, and "the lines of relationship run forth from ego in both directions, through males and females to the accepted limits of kinship...the *cognatio* surely defined a domain of affective ties as well." Herlihy observes that although Georges Duby describes the agnatic form supplanting the cognatic, the older form never completely dies out, and the two co-exist in the later middle ages.[36]

This combination of lineage types is a salient feature in Trevet's descriptions of Mary's immediate ancestors. These sections trace the marriages of sons and daughters, as well as their offspring. For example, in tracing the relations of Edmond, a son of Henry III, upon his being made Duke of Lancaster, Trevet writes:

"et esposa primes la fille le counte d'Aumarle [Albamarle, cf Danemark in ME] et son heir, et avoit de lui deux enfauntz qe morurent deinz age, et tost apres morust la countesse lour mere. Puis se maria a la reine de Nauvarre Blanche, la seor le count d'Artoys, et de lui avoit trois fitz Thomas, Henri et Johan. Cist Thomas estoit apres son pere counte de Lancastre, et prist a femme Aleyse, la fille et l'eir Henri de Lacy, counte de Nichole, et avoit par ceste Aleise deux countez, le countee de Nichole par son pere et le countee de Salesburs par sa mere, mes n'avoient emsamble nul heir. Henri, le frere cist Thomas, fu fait seignour de Monemewe [Mombray] par le doun Edmund son pere, et prist a femme la fille et le heir Patriz de Chaworthe, et de lui engendra un fitz Henri et sis filles, Blaunch, Isabel, Maude, Johane, Alianore, et Marie" (2.327.22–328–5).

he wedded furst the doughter of the Earle of Danmark and hys Eyre and he had by her III chyldren the whych died within age and anon after dyed the countes, her [their] moder. Than after this Edmond was wedded to quene of Navarn, Blanche the Suster to the Erle of Artoys and by her he had III sonnes, Thomas, Harry, and John. Thys Thomas was after hys fader Erle of Lancaster and took to his wife Alyse the doughter and eyre of Lacy Erle of Lincoln and he had by thys Alyse II erledoms. The earle-dom of Lincoln be her fader syde and the erledom of Salysbury by her moder syde but they had never none issew togeder. Than Harry the brother of thys Thomas was made lorde of Monemowe wedded Isabell the doughter and Eyre of Partyk of Chaworth and begate a son called Harry. And also he begate of her VI doughteres, Blaunch, Isabell, Maude, Jehane, Alianore, and Mary (355–56).

This section continues for another twenty-four lines of text tracing the marriages of these sons and daughters, as well as their offspring. Bound up in this list are accounts not only of political status but of dynastic marriage, procreation and property. Certainly many of the female figures are included because they are heiresses, but the text is exhaustive in recording the details of this family tree, explaining what happened to each of the people. Plantagenet women are not marginal here and do not exit the family tree. They bring important new alli-ances through their marriages, and their children remain actors in the family story.

Given the cognatic aspects of these family descriptions, it is not unreasonable to imagine an affective response on the part of these aristocratic readers to a description of their kindred and blood ties. Mary of Woodstock and her fellow readers may have felt profound re-cognition and pleasure at going over the family peerage. Mary would have found herself listed in such a sequence of royal marriages and births that appears between a narrative concerning the Welsh and Scottish campaigns and another explaining how Pope Innocent fol-lowed Pope Gregory.[37] Mary appears in this section of the chronicle three times. At the first, the primary topic is her father, King Henry, and his marriage. In a list of his offspring, Trevet points out Mary and her sisters with a cross-reference, "mes de cestes dirroms apres" (338) ["Bot of these daughters we woll say hereafter" (366)]. The second mention recounts the entrance of her grandmother into Amesbury in 1285, accompanied by Mary, then a young girl of seven or eight, and goes on to describe Mary's own taking of the veil.[38] Finally, Mary and all her sisters resurface in a section that elaborates upon each of them, their marriages and the births of their children. Like all parts of *Les Cronicles*, this section appears disjointed and very long to a modern reader, with only the barest connectives such as "then" or "and" weaving events together, and the phrase "Ci fest a retourner a l'engendrure le roi Edward, le fiz Henri avaunt dit" (2.350) ["nowe wyll we turne ageyn un to the engendrure of kyng Edward the son of Harry before sayde" (372)] somewhat arbitrarily introducing the discussion of the family. Through perusing the text, however, a medieval reader like Mary might re-read and recreate the lives of her own sisters and nieces and nephews. As she is herself included in this narrative:

> "La quarte fille fu dame Marie, de qi est avaunt dit qe se maria al haut roi de ciel, et en taunt est de li veritablement dit; "Optimam partem elegit sibi Maria, que non auferetur ab ea," qe fait taunt a dire; "La tres bone part s'en ad eslu Marie, qar cele part qe est Dieux meismes james ne lui tollet serra" (2.351).

> [the fourth doughter was dame Mary of whom it ys before sayde that she wedded herself unto the hygh king heaven. And in so moche as hit ys trewly sayde of her and notably this worthy text of holy scripture: *optimam partem elegt ipsi Maria que non auferetur ab ea*. The whych ys as moche to say "As Maria hathe chosyn the best party to her the whych shall not be done away from her"(374)][39]

The entry detailing Mary's life and her family's offspring is included in the middle of accounts of succession problems and the high politics of Edward I, as yet another item on a long, paratactic list of events and people. While the female figures in these genealogical lists are not emphasized, per se, neither are they subordinated. I would argue, however, that Mary and the other female readers of this history could take pride in finding their own lives situated within the retelling of great events performed by the "fellowship of men," that is agnatic lineage, and that they could find pleasure in seeing their own relatives and how they were connected spelled out within this national context, as persistent elements of cognatic lineage. Each reader, upon finding herself in the narrative, could construct her own *ego*, her own starting point in lineage and trace her blood relations cognatically through the pages of this history. Perhaps through the collected genealogical connections drawn by this chronicle, such readers could have imaginatively traced their line back through Matilda, the mother of the Plantagenets, to the figurative mothers of all Christians, Mary and St. Anne and their holy family. For these women, reading lineage could have offered them ways to identify with the figures of powerful women in the past, creating a sense of subjectivity that would give them a place in the political world.

Les Cronicles asserts the value of women's actions by presenting them as normative and essential to history. They are necessary to the success of family rule and to the reproduction of each new generation. Women who act in *Les Cronicles* do so with textual approval, serving an important narrative as well as historical function; they enable this history, so structured by genealogy and succession, to continue. The portrayal of Biblical and Plantagenet women offers intriguing possibilities for the women readers who were Mary of Woodstock's contemporaries and descendants, allowing them to see themselves or women like them written into the historical discourse of their day.

Each of these stories and genealogies is included side by side with the many stories of national conflicts, saint's lives, and the successions of kings and popes that fill this universal history. Let us turn now to the most extended treatment of a woman in *Les Cronicles*, its extraordinary centerpiece, the "Tale of Constance."

The "Tale of Constance": From Trevet to Chaucer

Study of the "Tale of Constance" has focused on Geoffrey Chaucer's late version presented in his *Man of Law's Tale*.[40] Examinations of Chaucer's primary source, *Les Cronicles*, however, neglect serious inquiry into the place of Constance within Trevet's work, failing to examine her story either as part of a larger, sprawling historical narrative that seeks to tell the history of the world from Biblical and Roman times, through ancient Britain, to the contemporary Plantagenets or as a story that is produced under the auspices of Mary of Woodstock, with her influence over its composition.

Chaucerians have long considered the tale to be simply the longest digression in Trevet's history, but it is, in fact, the central focus of *Les Cronicles*.[41] It occupies nearly the physical center of the text. Trevet's formulaic introduction to each chronicle entry changes from "l'an de grace" before the tale, to "l'an del Incarnation" after it, a change original to the author, since it appears in all manuscripts, including both Anglo-Norman and Middle English versions.[42] Two long genealogies, one before and one after, link the tale of Constance to a context of British and European history. In its central focus, the chronicle hinges on a problem of descent: the narrative must explicate Constance's story in order to explain how her reputed son becomes the Roman emperor after her father. Because the tale is so situated and emphasized within this coordinate, paratactic narrative, we must look at the tale as a chronicle entry,[43] and the figure of Constance in it, within the context of the chronicle as a whole.

If Mary of Woodstock, as I have argued above, was indeed involved in determining the content of this chronicle, with its emphasis on the stories of Biblical women and on the place of women in Plantagenet genealogies, the inclusion of Constance as a key link for the royal lineages of Europe would reinforce the political position of contemporary, medieval women readers. The figure of Constance, herself, could appeal to a Plantagenet woman's political interests. Throughout the story, in order to counter threats to her position, Constance engages in a process of self-creation that is essential to the completion of the story itself, bringing herself and her son to her father, the emperor, on her own terms. In the tale, a woman can be religious and politically active, yet act appropriately as a mother and queen.[44] As we examine Constance's insinuation of herself into Northumbrian society and the way she engineers her later, Roman recognition scenes, we find that she fulfills her political duties, creating international links through her marriage and continuity for the succession by providing a male heir. She does so, however, on her own terms, by selectively and strategically telling a version of herself, or by allowing a version told by someone else to go unchallenged to her own advantage. While she may begin as a traded, diplomatic bride, Trevet charts the process by which she becomes a subject in her own narrative, assuming control over her own genealogical place and the political ramifications this entails. She takes these roles and uses them, rather than passively accepting the status granted her by her position as the emperor's daughter, the wife of Alle, or the mother of Maurice.

As produced by Trevet and Mary of Woodstock, the figure of Constance and her place in history must be examined and worked through by the chronicle in order for history and the narrative to continue. Chaucer's Constance is known for her humble acceptance of her fate, but while critics remark that his Constance is more passive than Trevet's,[45] they fail to recognize that this transformation, effected by the added frame of the Man of Law as teller, essentially transforms the political message of Trevet's earlier work for the Plantagenet family, changing diametrically Mary of Woodstock's vision for women in dynastic politics.[46]

As noted above, genealogy structures Trevet's narrative throughout its encyclopedic compilation of the events of the world, providing cross-references for both familial and textual connections. Telling the story of Constance fits into but also explores and complicates this genealogical paradigm: her presence as Tiberius's daughter creates a gap in the succession and in the narration of lineage. After one of the longest genealogies in his chronicle, about 150 lines of the descent of Saxon kings and the popes, including a short digression relating Pope Gregory's meeting with some Anglian prisoners famously related by Bede, Trevet comes to the reign of the Emperor Tiberius and the succession of his heir, Maurice. But with this transition of power, the orderly passage of generations hits a crisis; it is not immediately clear how Maurice has gained the right to succeed Tiberius. Trevet could have been content with a conventional transition from grandfather to grandson and gone on to relate the history of Maurice's reign, but instead he puts aside his genealogical schema to excavate a subordinate tale that would explain Maurice's status and the seemingly missing generational puzzle piece.

By acknowledging Maurice as a grandson, therefore, the text brings the status of Constance, his mother, into focus since she is the actual genetic link that connects Maurice to Tiberius, and it is she who enables Maurice to take the object position as heir to the throne. He even becomes co-emperor, an unusual intermediate position between the subject and object spaces of the genealogical formula. Constance's story, therefore, must be told in order for Tiberius's lineage and the transition of royal power to be a strong one. In addition to solidifying the stages of Tiberius's lineage, Constance's marriage to the Northumbrian king Alle pulls together two sets of lineages that Trevet has stressed throughout his chronicle—the Latin and the Saxon as emphasized by the long Saxon genealogy immediately preceding this tale. Not just stylistically and structurally important to *Les Cronicles*, Constance's function as a link in lineage, both cognatically in Tiberius's and agnatically in Alle's, helps place Britain and British history in a larger world context. Although Northumbria is at first provincial and non-Christian, Constance's actions not only Christianize this part of Britain, but also connect it strongly to Rome.[47]

The possible meanings of Constance's marriage to Alle, however, go beyond the simple connections of a marriage alliance between two nations. The strange machinations surrounding the birth of her son

Maurice highlight an anxiety about lineage, reproduction, succession, status, nationality and race.[48] Telling Constance's story reveals a birth narrative that is seldom told in chronicle, explaining the feminine part in producing an heir and in creating and connecting lineage. Telling this tale also confronts the ways a foreign (and perhaps otherworldly) presence such as Constance's can threaten the interests of dynastic politics and the writing of history—because of Constance's marriages, the old order does collapse for Britain and for Syria, but it is solidified for Rome with the recognition of Maurice. Constance, like the Old Testament women whom Trevet has discussed earlier in the text, becomes an active component in her own lineage.

In Trevet, Constance is a difficult and marvelous figure for the people of Northumbria to interpret. Her strangeness is highlighted when she first arrives on their shores; she is described as a "merveil, c'est assavoir, un pucele de bele & genti affecture, mes descoloure, en strange atir et estoffe de grant tresour" (2.205.7–8) ["meruayle that ys to say a mayden full fayre and of a full ientell feture, but gretly discolored with a straunge atyre. And wele stored with full grete tresoure" (218)]. While Chaucer's Custance is incomprehensible upon her arrival in Northumbria, speaking only her own language, and claiming she does not know who she is for "she was so mazed in the see/ that she forgat hir mynde" (526–27),[49] Trevet's Constance herself guides the Northumbrians' reactions, manipulating circumstances so that they see her in terms of lineage and family. When Elda, the king's castellan, greets her "el lui respoundi en sessoneis... et lui disoit qe, quant a sa creance, ele estoit de cristiene foi; quant a linage, qe ele estoit de riches et nobles gentz estret, et qe par son linage estoit ele done en mariage a un grant prince, mes pur ceo qe ele desplut as grantes de la terre, pur ceo fu ele en tiele manere exile" (2.205.16–20) ["And she answered to hym and sayde that she was a Saxonesse and born in Saxon... And also that mayden seyde as for Creaunce and beleue that she was of the cristen feythe. And as touchyng her lynage she sayd that she was bore and bred of the ryght ryche folke and worthy. And be her langage she sayde that she was geuen in to Mariage vn to a grete prince. And for that cause that he mariage displeased the grete astates of that londe for that cause she was in suche maner exyled" (218–219)]. By telling Elda in Saxon that she is Christian and of noble lineage, Constance strategically leads him to hope, "esperoit" (2.205.25) or "suppose well" (219) in the Middle English, that she is the daughter of some German or Scandinavian king. He therefore treats her honorably, according to this assumed status. Constance herself deliberately crafts this identity—rather than the strange figure she initially presents, her reply causes her to be perceived as holding high status. This strategy allows the Northumbrians to overlook her near anonymity, as suits her purpose, since, "riens ne voleit reconustre de Tyberie, l'emperour son piere, ne del soudan, qar l'aventure del murdre del soudan et de les Cristiens estoit ja conue par totes terres" (2.205.20–23) ["she wold nat be aknowen of Tibery the Emperoure her ffader neyther of the Sowdan for the auenture of that morder of the sowdan and of the cristen men was then knowen thorow all londes" (219)].

Despite her marvelous arrival, Constance is accepted into the local aristocratic society, living with Elda and his wife Hermingild. The details of her reception and her time in Northumbria are crafted to produce two key events: the conversion of the Saxons to Christianity and the production of an heir. In a very brief but pointed incident, Elda tells King Alle about the mysterious woman in his household and these words inspire desire in Alle, a desire which is causative: "et quant le roi avoit touz cez ditz en privee conseil entre eux deux escote, mult fu desirous de la pucele veer et parler. Et a cest desir promist a Olda q'il privement le vindroit visiter" (2.208.10–13) ["whan the kyng had herkened all hys seying priuyly in counsayle betwyxt hem bothe, the kyng than desyred mych to see and speke with that mayde Constaunce and for that desyre he promysyd to Olda that he wold come pryuyly and to visite her" (222)]. Elda can tell Alle only what Constance herself has allowed him to know about her identity, that she is a Christian exile, presumably a Saxon princess. This knowledge, the identity that Constance, herself, crafted, prompts the king to visit her.

Constance's relationship with Alle continues to be narrated as a bare-bones, coordinate sequence in chronicle fashion. The king arrives at Elda's house, judges the vassel who has killed Hermingild, and "Puis le roi, pur le grant amour q'il avoit a la pucele et pur les miracles par Dieux moustrez, le roi Alle lui fist baptizer del evesque Lucius avant nome, et eposa la pucele, qe conceut del roi un enfant madle" (2.210.4–7) ["Than after the kyng for the grete loue that he had vn to that mayde and for the myracles shewed for her before god, Alle made hymself to be bapti3ed of the bysshop Lucius before named. And wedded that Mayden the whyche conceyued be her husbond kyn

Alle A son" (224)]. No connection is made explicitly between the king's earlier "desir" and his current "amour" and no event explains his love—it is only his love and the divine miracles that are offered as cause for the king to marry Constance. Constance's self-presentation sets a sequence of events in motion that culminates in a royal marriage, one that is almost synchronous with the conception of a royal child, who is explicitly named as male. By her act of creating herself, through speaking Saxon and deliberately leaving out detailed information about the circumstances of her exile, Constance has intervened in her own history and brought about events that make her a key player in the politics of lineage—the prospective mother of a royal heir who will connect the family lines and political histories of both Northumberland and Rome.

While Alle seems to have accepted Elda's interpretation of Constance as an exiled Saxon princess, his mother, Domild, has no such confidence in her daughter-in-law's status, illustrating the text's continuing ambivalence toward both the threat and the promise that foreign, dynastic marriage can bring. Envy is one reason for the Queen's enmity (a quality Gower makes the main focus of his version of this tale in the *Confessio Amantis*), but the first reason offered is her disdain: "et qe trop mortuement hey la reyne Constance; qar grant dedeyne avoit qe le roi Alla avoit pur l'amour une femme estrange et qui linage lui n'estoit pas conu; sa primer ley gurpi, quele touz ses auncestres avoient leaument et entierment gardez" (2.210.17–21) ["and the whyche hated dedly Constaunce the Quene, ffor she had full grete disdeyn and scorne that her son the kyng Alle shulde take a woman of a straunge londe. And moreouer that her linage and byrthe was nat knowen to her. And Also the kyng her son shulde forsake hys furst lawe, the whyche all hys Auncestirs had full entierly kept and holden" (224–25)]. Domild's refusal to accept Constance is explicitly explained as a dual problem of lineage—her own is patently unknown and she has caused the king to desert the heritage that his ancestors had passed down through the generations.

The anxiety that Constance's presence in Northumbria causes becomes further manifest when her son, Maurice, is finally born. This incident takes place immediately after the text spells out the grounds for Domild's suspicion and hatred: it is interpolated by the simple, coordinate conjunction *puis* [then]—"Puis quant Dieux et nature voleient, Constance fu delivres d'un enfaunt madle, bel et grant et bien engendre et bien nee, et al baptesme fu nome Moriz" (2.210.29–

30) ["than after whan god wolde and nature Constaunce was de-
lyuered of her fayre Chyle the whyche was a full fayre son. And wele
be geten and full well borne. And at the foonte stoone was named and
called Morys" (225)]. This is a matter-of-fact, ordinary event as the
phrase "quant Dieux et nature voleient" indicates; Constance's giving
birth is part of the course of things, but also an event that brings joy
for Elda and Lucius, who accept Constance's story, "hastivement
manderent novele graciouse al roi" (2.211.1) ["in all the haste that
they myght sente these gracious tydinges to the kyng Alle" (225)] of
the boy who is explicitly named as not only "bel and grant" but "bien
engendre et bien nee." For these participants, Maurice's lineage is beyond reproach and his birth is an event to be celebrated because the
king and country have a well-born heir.

　This birth tale, however, still takes place within the account of
Domild's distrust for Constance. The king's mother uses the birth of
Maurice as an opportunity to re-write the story of who Constance is
and what her family ties may be. In her extreme reaction, she creates
a version of Constance that makes her as different from the
Northumbrians as she can possibly be. When she intercepts and rewrites the letter of gracious news sent by Elda and Lucius to Alle
away at the Scottish wars, Constance is called "fu en manere et en
condicioun change en un autre creature, qar ele fu malveis espirit en
fourme de femme" (2.211.17–19) ["chaunged bothe in maneres and in
condicion as hit were all another creature. ffor she was aeuell spirite
in a wommans lykenes" (226)]. Not even a human being, the threat
that Constance represents to the bloodline of Northumbria and its
king is extreme. The heir to the throne is born as "ne resemble pas a
fourme de homme, mes a une maudite fourme hidouse et dolerouse"
(2.211.21–23) ["nat semblaunt to the lykenes of man but fourmyd and
syssape thyng to heuy and to shamefull to sey or to speke" (226)]. Because Domild casts Constance and her son in terms of extreme difference, it is clear that no familial or political link can be made by such
a marriage. Maurice becomes not the heir who will connect Britain to
Rome, but an impossible and unnatural link that must be destroyed.
Domild's subsequent machinations make sure that this takes place—
Constance and Maurice are, of course, once again set adrift in the
rudderless boat. Domild's intervention in the politics of lineage effectively displaces Constance's earlier shaping of herself and the role
that her interventive presence played in the national destiny of

Northumberland and its prospective connections to Rome. Her actions, however, illustrate the social anxiety instigated by queenly intervention; the unreasonable and extreme nature of her intervention creates a double censure. While she repudiates Constance's action and place, the text will repudiate hers.

Domild's fiction-making succeeds only in exiling Constance herself. Other listeners believe Constance's version of her tale and accept her space in their lineage and national history. However, it is not only the important male leaders of the kingdom who believe in Constance. It is also the Northumbrian people themselves, who on several occasions not only accept Constance, but act to confirm her social status. For instance, in explaining Domild's antipathy for Constance, the text describes the great esteem that both the rich and poor held for their queen. Apparently this esteem was such that there were "les chaunsouns qe les puceles de la terre fesoient et chauntoitent de lui" (2.210.27–28) ["the Maydenys made sones of Quene Constaunce. And euermore thorowgh the londe they songe Carolles of her" (225)]. Here exists a third, popular, version of Constance produced by the people, themselves. Their approval and acceptance confirm her status within the political entity her husband heads. The maidens read her story and respond to it with songs of their own, confirming her story and status. This *vox populi* also comes vividly to the fore after Domild succeeds in exiling Constance. Although the text does not place blame upon Alle for the exiling of his wife, for as the readers know, his orders to have Constance and Maurice held pending further investigation of their natures have been re-written by Domild, his own subjects, ignorant of Domild's part, censure his reputed actions. As he returns from the Scottish wars, "par citez et viles de jour en Engleterre, lui vindrent encountrauntz hommes et femmes, enfauntz et veillardz, et le revilerent de crie et ledeng, gettauntz sur lui et les seons tay et ordure et grosses peres, et femmes et enfauntz devestutz secucion qe lui covient et son ost desormes de nuyt prendre lour journeis" (2.215.15–21) ["And as the kyng wente and come by day by the hyghweyes by Cytees and by tounes in ynglonde there come men women and Chyldren and oolde folke crying and reuylyng the kyng and foule harlatrye opon hym with grete stones ayenst hys breste. And men wemen chylderen despoyled hemselfe naked for despyte, and shewed to hym her pryuytees behynde. And the kyng had so sore persecucion of hys pepull, that he must nedes take hys iorneys by nyght and nat by day" (231)]. This attack upon the king is unilateral and public; it occurs everywhere he goes and both genders and all ages participate in these actions. Where their songs of praise legitimate Constance's place as queen and mother of Alle's heir, the people's later actions come close to denying the legitimacy of Alle's government itself, all because he has seemingly denied and destroyed his wife and her generative role in perpetuating his political and national dynasty.

After her mother-in-law succeeds in exiling Constance and her son upon the open sea once again, Constance retains control over her representation by creating an equally mysterious and advantageous narrative when, back in the Mediterranean once more, she is discovered by Roman naval forces. Even though she recognizes the Roman leader who finds her, Arsemius of Cappadocia, he does not know her, an event which gives her "a grant joie"(2.217.7) ["toke hit to grete joy" (233)]. In this version of the tale, Arsemius's ignorance allows Constance to retain control over her own representation by once again selecting details from her past to craft an identity that is true, but singularly unrevealing. In response to his questioning, Trevet writes "et ele lui avoit sagement respoundu sanz rien descoverer de son linage ou del emperour" (2.217.11–12) ["she answered euer full wysely to hys axyng withoute any maner discoueryng of her lynage orelles of the Emperour her fader" (234)]. She not only hides her connections, but also conceals her immediate past, relating a story that is literally true, but too barren of specificity to be very revealing. As she says "ele estoit marie a une riche seignur qi avoit engendre l'enfaunt, a qi par sa fortune ele n'estoit pas pleisaunte en touz pointz" (2.217.14–16) ["she was maryed to a ryche lorde, the whyche had begote her son opon her to whom she was nat moste plesaunt in all poyntes" (234)]. She then cloaks her name, ironically by giving the true name she held in Northumbria, as "ele estoit Couste nome, qar issic l'apelerent les Sessoneis" (2.217.18–19) ["sayde that her name was called Conste, ffor so the saxons called her" (234)]. Constance retains control over her identity and over what people may say about her. Chaucer's version characteristically reduces this dialogue, reporting only that "ne she nyl seye/ of hire estaat, althogh she sholde deye" (972–73).

Constance even turns the tables on Arsemius, asking him about the surrounding navy. The meaning of the great military force is not transparent; when Constance first sees it she thinks it is a great forest, but as her ship approaches nearer, she recognizes the "trees" to be masts of ships. The meaning of the fleet, in fact, turns out to be another version of her own history. This force has slaughtered the Saracens who had set Constance adrift and killed her Christian entourage. This story specifically mentions the body of Constance which Arsemius sees before him and has failed to recognize. According to him, they were unable to re-inter the body of Constance with the other Christian victims because "solonc le dit de Sarazins estoit nee en la mere" (2.217.30) ["the whyche after the seying of the Sarazyns was drouned in the see" (234)]. This false report not only allows Constance to keep her anonymity, but also illustrates the benefit to her of doing so. By changing her name and concealing her history and connections, she creates a disjunction between who she is at present and the stories that are told of her, whether truly or falsely. In this process, she retains control over the telling of her own story, over the construction of her identity and over which familial and political connections she chooses to acknowledge or not.

It is only years after her arrival in Rome that Constance loses control over who she is perceived to be and even then she retains control over the process by which she is recognized. Although she almost swoons when she hears a report that Alle is to arrive at Rome and once again when she actually sees his face in a procession, Constance actively plans a conjunction of events that will reunite her with her husband. Once again the intervener in history,[50] Constance uses her blood tie with her son Maurice to reveal herself. As Trevet reveals her plan, Maurice "cist estoit apris privement de sa mere Constaunce qe, quant il irreit a la feste ove son seignur le senatur, qe, totes autres choses lessez, se meist devant le rois d'Engleterre" (2.219.20–23) ["Thys Mroyce was taught pryuyly of hys moder Constaunce that when he shulde go to the feeste with hys lorde the Senatoure that all thyng lefte he shall putte hymselfe before the kyng of Englond when that he were sette to hys mete" (236–37)]. Chaucer's only remnant of these detailed instructions is to mention that "som men wolde seyn at requeste of Custance/ this senatour hath lad this child to feeste:/ I may not tellen every circumstance —/ Be as it may, ther was he at the leeste" (1009–12), which seems an acknowledgement by Chaucer that he has minimized his heroine's role in these important events. In Trevet's version, however, Constance leaves nothing to chance, and her intention that Maurice's presence should reveal her own is clear, for Maurice should serve Alle "et qe de nule part se remuat hors del regard al roi, et qe il se afforsat bien et curteisement lui servir, qar il durement resembla sa mere" (2.219.23–25) ["And that in nowyse he remeued hymself fro the kynges syght. And that he serue hym wele and curteysly, ffor thys Moryce was passyngly lyke hys moder" (237)]. His body in its resemblence to his mother, reveals her body.

Although Carolyn Dinshaw argues that in this family bond, "the woman's image binds father and son, and later grandfather and [grand]son in what must be called the patriarchal gaze,"[51] her formulation minimizes the degree to which Constance has engineered this process of recognition and the link in lineage itself. Alle is a husband that her father did not choose. This version of her story illustrates how she takes and remakes for herself the place lineage has allotted to her. The chronicle as a whole uncovers the process by which women operate and are integral to lineage and generation, rather than burying it in a patrilineal genealogy. By sending Maurice to the feast, Constance, once again, tells her history and crafts her identity, but this time the signifiers are not words: she sends her son as a sign of herself. His signification is one of lineage—her maternal place in this narrative (and in Alle's life and political history) is revealed by the physical reality of her son's presence. As the mother of this boy who connects Britain and Rome, her place cannot be denied any longer, even perhaps by herself.

The recognition scene in which Alle sees Maurice is one of Trevet's most elaborately detailed pieces. Even though the people of Rome had, of course, long noticed Maurice's resemblance to Constance, because they have accepted Constance's vague explanation of herself, they have never seen its true significance. Once Alle sees Maurice, he is "trop fu surpris de la resemblaunce, et lui demaunda qi fitz il estoit, et il respoundi q'il estoit fitz Arsenie le senatur, qe lui seoit a destre" (2.219.26–29) ["bethought hym muche of hys resemblaunce. And axed hym whos son he was. And he ansered to hym full curteysly and seyde that he was the son of Arsenie the Senatoure whyche sate opon hys ryght hande" (237)]. While telling the truth as he knows it by acknowledging Arsemius as his adopted father, Maurice, like Constance, spins a tale that is literally true, but whose false implications would lead a listener into a blind, blocking further questioning and leading to a false conclusion. Alle, however, is not put off and turns further questions to Arsemius, who explains that Maurice was adopted as his son because he had lacked an heir. Arsemius can reveal only the vague and partial lineage that he knows for Maurice, the story of selected details that Constance has told him. As Trevet writes, Arsemius "sa mere savoit il bien mes noun pas son pere, qar unqe sa mere ceo ne lui voleit reconustre en le temps de duzze aunz; et le juvencel ne savoit, qar la mere et lui estoient mis en exil quant n'estoit for qe de dis semayns" (2.219.30–220.4) ["And hys moder wyst that full wele, but nat hys fader. ffor hys moder woulde neuer talle who was hys fader in all the tyme of thys xii yere. And Moryce knewe nat, for hys moder and he were exyled whan he was nat but x wokes of age" (237)]. This vague formula repeats Constance's version of her story.

It is clear that this story will not hold up under the scrutiny of a knowing listener such as Alle. No longer satisfied with vague connections, "le rois demaunda del juvencel son noun, et il respondi qe son non fu Morice" (2.220.4–5) ["Than asked the kyng of thys yong man what was hys name and he answered and seyde to hym that hys name was Moryce" (237)]. Alle is a reflective and insightful listener to this tale, for he takes time and goes over the information he has received and puts the pieces of the puzzle together: "dount lui devient en grant pensee et del noun et de la resemblaunce de visage et pur les ditz le senatur" (2.220.5–7) ["Than the kyng was in a grete thought and pensyfull bothe of the yong mannes name and of the semblaunce of hys vysage vn to hys wyfe hys oune moder. And also for the wordes of the Senatour the whyche he tooke good hede of before" (237)]. Presented in this way, as arranged by Constance for the knowledgable Alle, all signs lead back to Constance (for this is, in fact, a test for him) in her guise as his wife and as the mother of his son.

After such a detailed, planned, and slowly unfolded prologue, the actual recognition scene between Alle and Constance is short and public. After completing his reveree, Alle "demaunda del senatur si lui; lust faire moustraunce de la dame la mere le juvencel, et il lui respondi q'ele estoit en sa meson. sur ceo le rois trop confortee fist haster le manger" (2.220.7–10) ["And axed of the Senatoure yef that he knewe the chyldes moder, that hit myght lyke hym that he myght see her. And the senatoure answered to the kyng that the chyldes moder was in hys place there. And than the kyng hasted faste for to see her and hyed hym in all haste that he myght frome hys mete" (237)]. The recognition scene proper follows in typical, chronicle-like fashion, with a string of coordinate sentences, linked by "et": "Et quant il estoit descendu al paleis le senatur, parust sa femme, qe lui

venoit encountre ove la femme le senatur. Et le rois, apres q'il avoit la
dame del paleis salue, par certeine conoisaunce ala sa femme enbracer
et beiser. Et taunt apeert moustances d'amur ly fesoit, que le senatour
& la dame, et quanqe i estoient, ne estoient pas poi enmerveillez, et le
roi a ceo, tut en haut escrie, "J'ay trove ma femme!" (2.220.10–16)
["And than the Senatoure wente doune in hys paleys, and commaun-
ded hys wyfe to come doune with Constaunce in her moste goodly
atyre and aray to see the kyng. And assone as the kyng aperseyued
that lady Constaunce he salued her in hys moste goodly wyse. And be
full verey certeyn knowlache that anone he knewe her, he wente and
tooke hys wyfe Constaunce in hys armes and ofte tymes kyssed her.
And there the kyng shewed so opyn shewynges of hys loue vn to her
that the senatoure and hys wyfe and all tho, that were there meruey-
led muche thereof. And than the kyng with an hygh noyse and cry in
a hygh voyse sayde thus, 'I haue founde my wyfe'" (237–38)].

Chaucer's version, once again, highlights Custance's distress at
this development, portraying her as sorrowing and swooning twice
(1048–58). Chaucer does give some characterization not provided by
Trevet, explaining that Custance felt this way because she remem-
bered Alle's "unkyndenesse," in apparently ordering her out to sea
once again. The details of Trevet's scene, however, are spelled out in
detail, and for once, this chronicle comes to a definite conclusion
with an unusual exclamation when Alle cries out "j'ay trove ma
femme." He has found his wife and publicly acknowledged her social
place, her identity, and her place within his lineage. This position is
accepted and acknowledged both socially and politically, since Alle is
attended by his castellan Elda and the Bishop Lucius, who both greet
Constance with joy and praise to God at her recovery.

In staging this recognition scene, Constance has intervened in
events and recouped part of her social and narrative place. Her largest
significance, however, is to link the histories of Rome and Britain—
this is an aspect of her identity, unknown to Alle that has yet to be
revealed: she is the daughter of the emperor, an identity which is
masked by the story of the Saracens' slaughter and her reputed death
in that incident.

In a series of events that nearly replays her earlier plans for Maurice to approach Alle, Constance arranges for not only herself, but for
her entire family unit to be recognized by the emperor. Her new identity will supplant the rumor of her slaughter at the hands of the

Saracens. This final episode in the tale places Constance in the active, subject position; she controls and creates the story. Constance first "un nuyt lui pria Constance q'il maundast al emperere... q'il vousist lui faire l'onur q'il lui plust ove lui manger a Rome" (2.220.22–24) ["prayed hym [Alle] that he would vouchesafe to sende to the Emperour Tiberie... that he would do to hym the worshyp for to com and to dyne with hym at Rome" (238)]. Having attained Alle's consent, Constance next "charga son fitz Moriz del message, et lui dist; Si l'emperour ne lui grantast point sa priere, qe dunqe lui requeist pur l'amur q'il avoit al alme sa Constaunce" (2.220.25–28) ["charged her son Moryce with the message and seyde to hym, that he shulde pray the Emperour opon the kynges of ynglond behalue that hit myght please hys hyghness to come dyne with hym. And yef the Emperour wolde nat graunt to hys prayer, that than he shulde require hym for the loue that euer he had to the soule of hys doughter Constaunce" (238)]. Not only are her instructions to her son once again quite detailed, her own authority is also doubled—she initiates and plans this encounter, and even brings it about by invoking the image of herself in yet another guise, the dead and saintly daughter.

Constance picks the precise time and place for this meeting and once her father appears, she takes the final initiative when she "pria son seignur de descendre de son destrer encountre l'emperour... Et Constaunce devaunt tote la compaignie prist son seignur le roi en la mein destre et Moriz son fitz en la meyn senestre, et vient son pere saluer en cestes paroles; 'Mon seignur et beau pere Tyberie, jeo, Constaunce vostre fille, mercie Dieux qe encore a ceste jour m'ad graunte la vie, qe jeo vous vei en saunte'" (2.221.15–21) ["prayed the kyng that he would vouchesafe to alyghte of hys steede ayenst the Emperour the whych ded so. And than Constaunce before all the company tooke her lorde in her ryght hande, and she come and kneled doune and salued her fader by these wordes. 'My lorde and my fayre fader Tiberie. I Constaunce your doughtre thanke hyghly our lorde god, that yet at thys day hathe graunted to me my lyfe that I may see youre nobull persone in helthe'" (239)]. Constance reveals herself in the strongest possible terms. Constance, her true name, and the phrase "vostre fille," her hitherto hidden familial and political connection, are syntactically equated with "ieo" an active subject of the narrative who has created this scene and who makes the utterance that gives it a climactic and revelatory significance. As Tiberius's daughter, she connects Britain and Rome, a connection she has herself forged by marrying Alle and by literally bringing all of her male relations to-gether.[52]

All of the tales told of Constance and which Constance has told of herself come together in this final tableau. She recreates visually her sojourn in Northumbria, and once her father has seen her and recovered from his swoon, "et Constaunce conta a son pere totes ces aventures et coment ele avoit ja douze anz demore en la meson le senatur Arsenie" (2.221.25–27) ["And than Constaunce tolde her fader all her auentures, and howe she had dwelled x yere in the house of the senatoure Arsenie" (239)]. These recapitulated stories replace for the emperor the version of Constance in which he believed. In fact, in his mourning for the supposedly dead Constance, he had appropriated her life's story, never eating or making merry, and granting all petitions if they were made with an appeal to his daughter's soul. He has become defined relationally as well, as the mourning father of a slaughtered daughter. When Constance presents herself as a conscious and living first person subject, she takes back her life's story—no longer traded to the Saracens or a dead relic of family politics, she inhabits the powerful narrative position of queen and wife and mother not only of Alle's son, but of the new heir to Rome.

When Constance proclaims herself "Jeo, Constaunce, vostre fille" to Tiberius, and her Roman family accepts her as such, she does more than just intervene in the processes of narrative and history to create her own identity. The identity she claims and forges is an important one, one that not only links the politics and lineages of Britain and Rome, but also links and brings together Trevet's version of her tale, enmeshing it within his greater chronicle. After her self-identification, the chronicle entry again picks up its initial emphasis—how Maurice became the next emperor of Rome after Tiberius and why he is the legitimate heir. As Trevet writes: "quant le roi Alle s'en voleit retourner en son pais, l'emperour Tyberie, par assent le pape Pelagie et de tut le senat de Rome, pur sa veilesce prist Moriz compaignon del emperour, et lui clama son heir" (2.221.29–222.2) ["whan the kyng Alle returned ageyne homewarde in to ynglond. The Emperour Tybery by the assent of pope Pelagy and of the Senat of Rome for cause of hys age toke Moryce hys doughter son for to be hys felowe to gouerne the Empyre. And made hym to be called hys Eyre apperaunt" (239–40)]. The emperor may convey the actual political power of designating an heir, but this act is predicated on the story of Constance and the unpredicted fate of her reproducing body.

Once the story of Constance is complete, this chronicle remains concerned with who Maurice is and how and why he succeeds Tiberius, calling him "Christianissimus Imperator," and taking up the story of his marriage and his reign. But in order to explicate Maurice's narrative place, the chronicle must excavate the complex narrative role his mother Constance has played both in bearing him at all and then in finally bringing him forward to succeed to the throne of Rome. If Constance had not sought recognition, Maurice would never have become heir to Tiberius. Only through a textual exploration of Constance's pursuit of and control over her identity, her story and her place in lineage can we find that the emperor Maurice is both of Northumberland and of Rome.

The "Tale of Constance" is the narrative, structural, and thematic centerpiece of *Les Cronicles*. The figure of Constance and her story combine two emphases from the chronicle as a whole: as a daughter, wife, and mother, she is a genealogical link between lineages, and she intervenes in the political processes of succession. Her feminine narrative presence and activity are necessary to the progress of this history, but even though this narrative sometimes makes her an object, her self-presentation often allows her to occupy the subject postition. As Trevet crafts his history to explore gender, Constance crafts her own identity and life's story to further her own survival and social place.

Nicholas Trevet crafted his text both for Mary of Woodstock and possibly according to her preferences and beliefs. He created a chronicle that offers a model of history which includes women as important players and narrative links. This narrative foregrounds important Biblical women, privileges the matriliny of the holy family, and places a politic treatment of the Plantagenet family, including women in its lists, within this narrative context. These emphases become focused in the tale of Constance, the story of a woman whose journeys are framed by genealogy. In this episode, the progress of history is halted by a problem of descent; only exploring gender and explicating Constance's place will allow the narrative to continue, creating the story of an active heroine creating her own history, most unlike Chaucer's

Man of Law's Tale, with its pale Custance, floating in her ruddlerless boat.

Mary of Woodstock and Nicholas Trevet, as patron and author, produced this family history for the Plantagenets, a courtly reading audience. By regularly inserting women in recountings of lineage, both Biblical and Plantagenet, and by explicating the position of Constance within her Northumbrian and Roman families, *Les Cronicles* allowed an aristocratic woman like Mary of Woodstock to display her power and to preserve a record of women's political and familial status for her descendants and their peers to read. By including accounts of active women in national history, texts such as *Les Cronicles* offered women opportunites to validate their social roles, as well as to interrogate their often contradictory positions within medieval culture's social, political, and economic institutions.

Reading the Past in 1400: *Sir Gawain and the Green Knight* and the Middle English Prose *Brut* Chronicle

ir Gawain and the Green Knight* begins with lines that situate it as an event in the history of Britain, within a further context of a Trojan past. Later in the poem, the anonymous author claims the "Brutus bookes" as his source for the story of the other-worldly testing of Gawain and of Arthur's court. Most scholars assume the poem's conception of this past to have been formed by the works of Guido della Colonne and Benoit de Sainte Maure.[1] As we have seen, however, the tradition of Geoffrey of Monmouth's *Historia regum Britanniae* was far reaching and dynamic. A late version of Geoffrey's history, the Middle English prose *Brut*, is contemporary with the *Gawain*.[2]

The prose *Brut* chronicle, like its predecessors, organizes time as the production of generations, but in a marked shift from its textual history, resists interruptions of that schema. Rather than using outcast or female figures to probe systems of inheritance or marriage, as did earlier texts, the prose *Brut* expresses at best ambivalence toward these figures—either appropriating any authority they have within the structures of genealogy or portraying them as wildly transgressive and worthy of condemnation. In the opening story of Albine and her sisters, Britain is founded by exiled women who have killed their husbands. Although Brutus soon arrives to destroy their monstrous offspring and re-establish Britain with Trojan settlers, an unruly female presence resurfaces though the years of the chronicle. The feminine ultimately becomes associated with the threatening presence of foreign figures in England, with the text, as a result, fixing much of the blame for the nation's political problems on the practice of exogamous marriage.

When we read the *Gawain* in the context of a history such as the *Brut*, we find the marginalization of female figures in both texts. In *Sir Gawain and the Green Knight*, however, the genealogical structure of history is still used to authorize the social tests created by a figure like Morgan Le Fay. This romance, while partaking of the kind of invective against women seen in the *Brut*, still uses the dual narrative form of genealogical history and romance found in the *Historia regum Britanniae*, which remained in circulation at this time. In this context, Morgan's role, conflated with Mary's, confounds the social identity of the Arthurian court by accessing the authority that succession narratives vest in reproducing female figures. This shift in the treatment of gender and history in these two late-fourteenth-century texts would appear to indicate significant changes in the kind of gendered positionings that could be presented to medieval readers and could also indicate changes in the options courtly women had for participating in the production of culture.

Women in the Early Sections of the Prose *Brut*

The prose *Brut* associates female figures more with social disruption and difference than with the power of social legitimization evinced in earlier historical texts in this tradition. Anne Bergren argues that sexual reproduction grounds women's narrative and political power. Since only they are in a position to name the father of a child, by providing true statements or difficult to discern false ones, their ability to produce signs, in the form of both words and future generations, is authorized and yet thrown into question by its grounding in reproduction. Thus "the production of social legitimacy is in her hands."[3] Although male discourse tries to appropriate this ability, patriarchy's power to control this process can often be quite limited. In Bergren's work, these complex valences of women's access to power and their ability to signify in the political and familial discourses of history are part of what gets traded with a bride in the formation of marriage alliances.

Because of their place in marriage alliances, Bergren argues that the figures of traded women draw many different anxieties about difference in terms of nation, blood, ethnicity, and race. In historical and mythic discourses, such marriages can become the "origin" of conflict and the mark of a foreign presence. Louise Fradenburg argues similarly that medieval queens could be "plastic figures" and their access to power gave them a kind of liminality that could mark cultural and discursive power in a process of negotiation. In other words, queens' roles in history can seem to be out of the ordinary and may become associated with change because they "emerge with special force at moments of crisis, of 'passage,' when rulers are marrying, dying, or being born, taking or losing power."[4] Women's extraordinary status and association with political crises occurs because under ordinary circumstances, that is, when generations proceed smoothly, guaranteeing that patriarchy seems a "natural" system,[5] women's ability to legitimate reproduction is not required and may be successfully buried and appropriated. But at critical junctures for political succession or questions of national identity, a woman's speech and body must be brought out to foreground this process of legitimization. This positions women in sites of difference and cultural strife, with Parsons describing the queen's body as a "site of crossover between cultures and spheres of power" in his study of royal rituals.[6]

Although Geoffrey of Monmouth's concern with gender and his storytelling skill are condensed in this later version of Britain's early history, some tantalizing incidents remain with even more interesting additions. We will first examine the foundation story of Albine to determine how the *Brut* blames Britain's troubled history on its origin in a failed and violent marriage alliance and attempts to supplant that origin with the more acceptable Brutus tale. In this version, other prominent figures from Geoffrey's history have lost their legitimizing force as well. To conclude the discussion of the *Brut*, we will examine how this history associates the foreign with the feminine as the cause of Britain's troubled history in a series of foundation stories and the Saxon incursion into Britain.

In the Prologue to the story of Brutus's travels, Britain is settled by Albine and her thirty-two sisters, all daughters of Diocletian, a king of Syria. These daughters create a crisis in the historical narrative when they rebel against the marriages made for them by Diocletian and kill their husbands. As punishment, they are sent by ship to exile on the empty isle of Britain. There, they produce monstrous children from a union with Satan.

Initially, the marriages of Diocletian's daughters are presented as an enhancement to his prestige and actual political power. For not

only was Diocletian a "noble kyng and myghty, & a man of grete re-
noun," but he "wel and worthily hym gouernede, & rewlede thurgh
his noble chiualrye, so that he conquered alle the landes abowte hym,
so that almoste all the kynges of the world to hym were enten-
daunt"(1).[7] Diocletian's asset of thirty-three daughters who "whan
they comyn in-to Age, bycomen so fayre that it was wondyr," is the
result of his own reasonable and controlled, endogamous marriage to
Labana, "a gentyl damysele that was wondyr fayr, that was hys Eemys
doughter, Labana" (1). Because of these political and domestic bless-
ings (the text says "wherfore"), Diocletian decides to hold a feast, a
public recognition and enactment of his power as he "anon lete make
A sompnyng, & comundid by his lettres that All the kyngys that
heldyn of hym schulde come at A certayn day...the feste was ryally
Arayd; & there they lyved in ioy and merthe y-now, that it was wonder to wete" (1). This feast culminates in the marriage of the thirty-
three daughters to the gathered kings, sealing alliances and consoli-
dating the political power of their father.

What should be a fairly standard account of a patriarch's political
maneuvering, however, becomes completely undercut by the subsequent actions of Albine and her sisters. They prove to be unruly
wives, unwilling to recognize the sovereignty of their new husbands.
Although she is queen of her own land, "dame Albyne bycome so
stoute & so sterne, that sche told litel prys of her lord, And of hym
hadde scorne and dyspite, and wolde not done his wylle, but wolde
haue here owne wyll in diuerses maners" (2). The other thirty-two
sisters behave in a similar manner because, as the text explains, they
"thought that here housebondes were not of so hye parage comen as
here fadyr" (2). The text details at length the outrageous behavior of
the women and their husbands' attempts to reform them with "fayr
speche," gifts, warnings and finally beatings. But it was "for nou3t, for
they deden her owne wil in all thyng that hem lykede & hadde of
power" (2). The status of these women as the king's daughters is completely at odds with the expectation that they serve husbands and be
queens of countries that do not equal their father's standing.

In desperation, the husband of Albine and his compatriots in domestic misery dispense letters to Diocletian, appealing to his authority to contain the unruly behavior of his daughters. Paradoxically,
however, his authority and status is precisely the problem. When the
families gather once again at a feast held by Diocletian, he "he spak

vn-to hem of here wikkydnes & of here cruelte, & dispitously hem reproued...sayde that, ȝif thei woulde not be chastised, thei schulde his loue lese for euermore" (3). The daughters are momentarily abashed and swear that they will make amends, but upon gathering again in their chamber, Albine tells her sisters "ful weel ȝe knowith that the kyng oure fadir, vs hath reprouyd, schamed & dispised, for encheson to make vs obedient vn-to oure housbandes; but certes that schal y neuere, whiles that I lyve, seth that I am come of a more hyere kynges blod than my housband is" (3). Albine uses the very blood connection that "the kyng oure fadir" hopes will compel obedience, to overturn his request and justify her subsequent actions. The sisters choose to murder their husbands that very night in their beds, for it was "better we mowe do this thing vndir our fadres power than elles-where" (3). Rather than solidifying his social power, the marriages of Diocletian's daughters have created social chaos—women have killed their husbands and kings, leaving domestic and political crises throughout Diocletian's sphere of influence. Ironically, the daughters have done this through the very status they enjoy and refuse to relinquish as his offspring.

This social standing continues to benefit the sisters for even when their father "bycome hugely wroth A-ȝens his Doughtres, & anon wolde hem all haue brent" (3), it is the barons and lords themselves that counsel mercy in the form of exile. The king should not kill his own children and cut off his own family line. The nobles who counsel mercy nonetheless insist that Diocletian "schulde voide the land of hem for euermore, so that thei neuere schulde come aȝen" (3). But the text itself explicitly judges and punishes these unruly women through their exile in England. These women are banished from the land of their family and birth; their contradictory use of kinship pollutes its future and that of Diocletian's race.

Albine's first action upon reaching dry land is to give the island her name—Albion—a naming agreed to by all the sisters. However, the fate of the sisters becomes clear as they explore the island. After they take possession of it, "thei went vp and doun, and founde neither man ne woman ne child, but wylde bestes of diuers kyndes" (4). There is no human civilization, no law or family here to govern these women. After their supplies run out, the women begin to dine on the native "erbes & frutes in seson of the ȝeer" (4). They do not cultivate plants or animals, instead living off the bounty of Albion. But the text does not allow such an Edenic narrative to continue for long, for "after that, thei tokyn flessh of diuers beestys, and bycomen wondir fatte, and so thei desirid mannes cumpanye" (4). This wild existence, living outside law and civilization, has brought out their animal nature. They eat gluttonously and so become fat, which seemingly triggers an unquenchable sexual desire. The text represents their situation as desperate: "and mannys kynde that hem faylled; and for hete they woxen wondir coraious [lustful] of kynde that hem faylled, so that they desirid more mannys cumpanye than eny other solas or merthe" (4). These women who would not submit to the control of their husbands or their father, are now completely out of control in the throes of gluttony and desire for the "kynde" whom they have killed and who have banished them.

This ominous development leaves the women open to the punishment that the narrative has devised for them:

> Whanne the Deuyll that perceyued and wente by diuers contres, & nome [took] bodyes of the eyre & likyng natures shad of men, & come in-to the land of Albyon and lay by the wymmen, and schad tho natures vpon hem, & they conceiued, and after thei broughten forth Geauntes, of the which on me called Gogmagog, and another Laugherigan. (4)

Sexual desire literally leaves them prey to the Devil's work, in a way that aptly shows the consequences of their behaviors. These women who have overturned their father's attempts to create political and social alliances through legitimate marriage, have peopled their society with monstrous offspring. Their legacy is a perverse genealogy. Although they have undercut their father's genealogical enterprise, their crimes are visited back upon them. The giants become the faded image of the women, since "they dwellyd in Cauys & in hulles at here will & had the lond of Albyon as hem liked" (4). Because the daughters of Diocletian had their will and did "as hem liked" the text reduces them to something less than human. The text associates these regal, yet unruly daughters with wild and uncontrollably foreign creatures.

This is not a fortuitous beginning for the history of Britain. But the *Brut* proper begins immediately with an alternative and more acceptable origin for Britain, the adventures and rehabilitation of the Roman/Trojan hero Brutus. Although his story is greatly reduced from its full treatment in Geoffrey Monmouth's *Historia regum Britanniae*, the elements that parallel the story of Albine and her sisters remain. Brutus is an exile who has committed an unpardonable blood crime, killing not a spouse, but his own father and mother. Through his campaigns to liberate the Trojans he finds in Greece, and his subsequent travels and military exploits in the Mediterranean and France, however, Brutus is explicitly rehabilitated and becomes a great leader and patriarch of a new Trojan-descended bloodline. His goddess Diana points him to Britain, telling him to "go euenforth thy wey ouer the see in-to Fraunce toward the west, & ther 3e schul fynde an ile that is called Albyon. .. in that lond were wont to be Geaunt3; but it is not so but al wyldirnesse; and that lande to 3ou is destynyed, & ordeigned for 3ow & for 3oure peple" (8). This destiny is not easily attained, for Brutus and his originary narrative must supplant and replace the earlier narrative of Albion: the giants, legacy of Diocletian's out-of-control daughters, still live there when Brutus arrives, and they contest his easy occupation of the island. The text describes the attack of the giants in great detail, especially the hand-to-hand combat of Gogmagog and Brutus's chief ally, Corinus.

After this victory over the giants, Brutus divides the island among his people and renames them both after himself: "Brut lete Calle al this land Britaigne, after his owne name, & his folk he lete calle Britouns" (12). British history can now be told in proper patriarchal terms—stories of great, lawgiving rulers and the sons who succeed them. Just as Brutus's name replaces Albion's, so his story takes authoritative control of the historical narrative.

This replacement and rehabilitation is not completely effective, however. Certainly the name of Albion for the island persists, but through later female figures, this story of the origins for Britain remains to be re-enacted again and re-silenced, instead of simply being left out of the narrative altogether. This alternate origin, recording how the sisters undercut their father's familial and social authority, serves to undermine and threaten the historical and legitimizing pretensions of the prose *Brut*. Like Morgan Le Fay in *Sir Gawain and the Green Knight*, women who would have their own will surface time and again through this history.

Although the problematic story of Albine is not included in Geoffrey Monmouth's *Historia regum Britanniae*, the rest of the first quarter of the *Brut* text closely parallels this source. The linear progression of generations remains an important structuring device. Chapters are often no more than brief entries in a genealogy, for example, chapter eight: "After the deth of Kyng Ebrac, regnede Brut Greneshel, his sone xxx 3er, that was Ebrakes ferst sone, that wel and noblye regnede. and when tyme come, he deide, and lith at 3ork" (15). The anonymous author of the *Brut* often condenses incidents that Geoffrey examines in depth, and in doing so, minimizes the impact or power female figures may have upon critical political situations. For instance, in the political crisis precipitated by Locrinus's setting aside his wife Gwendolyn of Cornwall for the captured German princess Estrilde, the text preserves the outrage of Cornyn, Gwendolyn's father, but makes a key change. The threat posed by the foreign princess Estrilde is negated when she herself negotiates for peace, for when Cornyn "drow his fauchon an hye, and wold haue slayn Lotryn, but the Damysell went be-twen hem, & made hem acorded in this manere, that Lotryn schuld spouse Guentolen" (13). Even though Lotryn maintains a clandestine affair with Estrilde, the text leaves out any description of outrageous behavior on the part of Gwendolyn. She merely repairs to Cornwall, and from there, attacks Lotryn, eventually killing him, Estrilde, and their child. These actions are depicted as reasonable and rational responses to her husband's infidelity. And as in Geoffrey, she remains a good regent for her son, governing "the land ful well & wysely" (14). The political threat posed by these two women is greatly contained in this account. While neither is explicitly condemned by the text as are Albine and her sisters, their more willful actions from Geoffrey's *Historia* have been erased in this text.

When retelling the story of King Leir, the prose *Brut* offers a perfunctory account of Cordelia that minimizes the radical political importance she held in Geoffrey of Monmouth's history as the only woman to rule Britain in her own right. After Leir's test, Cordelia is married to the King of France because he has heard that she "was wonder faire, and of so goode condicions and maners" (17). Eventually, he and Leir reach a bargain in which France will gain "oneliche heir clothing and oneliche heir body" (17). This account shares with Geoffrey the denial of dowry and marriage alliance, but leaves out the King of France's reasons for wanting Cordelia's body—" ut heredes ex illa haberet" (Griscom 265) ["so that he might have children by her" (Thorpe 83)]. In this version, the merit of Cordelia's royal bloodline in the genealogical project is de-emphasized. Her portrayal is that of a more traditional, inactive woman and traded bride, in spite of the contrary spirit she shows when answering her father's famous question.

Even when this Cordelia rules Britain, she is a pale figure compared with Geoffrey's queen. Throughout the story, she has been defined by her familial ties to men, as Leir's daughter, France's wife, and finally his widow. When her nephews rebel against her rule, it is not because they are outraged to be ruled over by a woman, as in Geoffrey, but that they "to here hade enuy, for-asmiche that her aunt shulde haue the lande" (20). Cordelia is marked only by her familial role as their aunt. She remains a passive figure in the plot when the nephews "vppon here werrede gretlich," and "thai hade here taken, and put her vnto deth" (20–21).

Surprisingly, the *Brut* also ignores the performances of women whose virtues are exemplary. Helen is indeed named as a saint and described briefly as an asset to her son, Constantine ("he toke with him his moder Elyn, for the michel wisedome that she couthe" [40]). Marcia, to whom Geoffrey and other early British historians attribute the writing of the Mercian Code, is mentioned only in passing. The role of the daughter of Claudius, here named Gennen, is reduced as well. She inspires no great love in her civic-minded husband Armoger, as in the *Historia regum Britanniae*, and no mention is made of the peace that she negotiated between her husband and her father.

A striking example of this reduction in the tales of virtuous women is the story which in Geoffrey's *Historia* seems to answer that of the violent Judon [Ydoyne in the *Brut*], that of Tonuvenna, the mother of Belinus and Brennius. In the middle of her sons' civil war, the *Brut* relates that "heir moder Cornewenne, that tho Leuede, herde that the o brother woulde haue destroyede that othere, and went bituene here sones, and ham made accordede with miche peyne" (26). Gone is Geoffrey's dramatic detail of the mother who bares her breasts before her sons' armies and exhorts them in direct speech to forsake their conflict and find equality as her offspring.

While the *Brut* has minimized the roles of some of Geoffrey of Monmouth's more politically intervening female figures, it vigorously censures the actions of women who act against the interests of succession. Goneril and Regan, for instance, are explicitly condemned for crimes against the royal line. As the Leir story enters its second phase, the text relates that "thus it bifel afterwarde, that tho ii eldest doughtren woulde nouȝt abide til that Leir here fader were dede, but werrede oppon him whiles that he leuede" (18). While Geoffrey places the blame for this rebellion on Leir's sons-in-law, the Dukes of Albany and Cornwall, the prose *Brut* describes the situation in more general terms, not involving the dukes in Leir's overthrow, and by never mentioning specific battles or describing who led troops against Leir. Here the crime is a strictly genealogical one; Goneril and Regan are his heirs, but they twist the royal line by not waiting for his death to take control. They war on their father while he is still alive. As quoted above, the text implies that the daughters should wait for Leir's death. Their actions are implicitly condemned as unnatural and out of control, much like the rebellious actions of Albine and her sisters.

Coming close on the heels of the Leir story is the vivid narrative of Ydoyne, the mother who killed her son. The text not only preserves Geoffrey's portrayal of Ydoyne as an unbalanced woman, it also expands upon that portrayal and offers explicit and vehement condemnation of her actions. The text does not explain her actions as madness, or characterize them as vengeance. For the prose *Brut*, these actions are inexplicable and can only be reported: "When Ydoyne, here moder, wist that Porrex was dede [names of the brothers are reversed from Geoffrey's account], she made grete sorwe, for enchesoun that she louede him more than that othere and pou3t him forto quelle" (22). Her sorrow can be attributed to her great love, but no reason or justification is implied for her plotting to kill her other son. Immediately following—"priuely she come to here sone oppon a ny3t with ii knyfes, and therwith cotte his throte, and the body also into smale pecis" (22). Here Ydoyne acts alone, while in Geoffrey's *Historia*, she works in concert and perhaps shares responsibility with her two maids. In a text that truncates its source and relates stories in little detail, this action has been amplified with more, gory detail added (Geoffrey writes only that she hacked him to pieces). But the most startling addition follows when the narrative directly addresses the reader with a rhetorical question, asking "who herde euer soche a cursede moder, that quellede with here owen hondes here owne sone!" (22). The text then explicitly condemns Ydoyne, and perhaps any woman like her, saying "and Longe tyme after laste the reprofe & shame to the moder that, for enchesoun of that o sone, mordrede that othere, and so loste ham bothe" (22). Like Geoffrey's *Historia*, the *Brut* points out that this is a genealogical crime. Because of Ydoyne's actions, "when thise ii bretherne were so dede, thai nade Lefte bihynde ham noo sone ne doughter, ne none othere of the kynrede that might haue the heritage" (22). The narrative does not leave out this example of threatening feminine behavior, but is instead fascinated by it, embellishing the crime's detail to make it even more beyond the pale. The story of Ydoyne must be repeated so that it may be even more strongly condemned and suppressed. This tale functions, however, as a trace of Albine, of women who disrupt the genealogical project with its illusion of social stability that the writing of history wishes to attribute to patriarchy in order to legitimate it.

The treatment of women in the early section of the prose *Brut* remains perfunctory, especially when compared to the *Historia regum Britanniae*. Women who provide legitimization within genealogical structures are suppressed and their voices are never really exploited for political or narrative advantage. Only female figures who seem to threaten patriarchal order are singled out for detailed treatment and ringing condemnation. This pattern continues, but becomes somewhat more complex in the second section of the text, from Arthur through the early Plantagenets, when the text turns its attention more toward marriageable women who bring political assets, but whose foreign connections can threaten a British monarch. These foundation stories connect women to anxieties about difference and link them to foreign influences in Britain that this history paints as challenging the nation's integrity as a people of one blood.

Britain, Marriage, and Foreign Brides

Toward the end of its history, during the reign of Edward II, the *Brut* describes an England warring against itself, using the terminology of family relations:

> the land tho was withouten Law, for holy cherche tho hade nomore reuerence than hit hade bene a bordel hous. And in that bataile was the fader aʒeins the sone, and the vncle aʒeins his nevew; for so miche vnkyndenesse was neuer seyne bifore in Engeland amonges folc of on nacioun; for o kynrede had no more pite of that other, than an hundred wolfes haueth on o shepe; and hit was no wonder, for the grete lordes of Engeland were nouʒt all of o nacioun, but were mellede with othere nacions, that is forto seyn, somme Brions, somme Saxones, sommes Danois, somme Peghtes, somme Frenchemen, somme Normans, somme Spaignardes, somme Romayns, some Henaudes, some Flemngus, and of othere diuerse naciouns, the whiche nacions acorded nouʒt to the kynde bloode of Engeland. And if the grete Lordes of Engeland hade bene onelich wedded to Englisshe peple, than shulde pees haue bene, and reste amongus ham, withouten eny envy. (220)

The nation is depicted as various kindreds each with their own ethnic loyalties, with fathers and sons, uncles and nephews, tearing the nation apart like wolves among sheep. Earlier histories commonly describe the fall of Britain in ways that emphasize the breaking down of the social fabric, but the *Brut* does not blame only a lack of religion or church power. As the passage above illustrates, this history explicitly cites the marriage practices of the aristocracy as the cause of this unrest. By practicing exogamous marriage, that is marrying foreign women, the text claims that these lords have been "mellede with othere nacions" and that if they had "onelich wedded to Englisshe peple," or practiced endogamous marriage, the resulting homogeneity would guarantee an England at peace.[8]

In a series of foundation stories, we see endogamy emphasized. Scotland and Ireland are established in tales that parallel the wanderings of Brutus and his band of Trojan exiles but that connect the establishment of these nations to the politics of marriage. In its insistence on endogamous marriage, the text links distrust of foreigners to its earlier condemnation of women who play active roles in the narration of history. Exogamy, however, was the dominent practice of the British kings, and the text's preference for endogamy is often undercut by the necessity of marriage alliances and the need for producing new generations to insure the succession.

The first of these short foundation narratives explains the settlement of Ireland. In Geoffrey's earlier text, based on Nennius's account, the British king Gurguit Barbtruc encounters wandering exiles from Spain in thirty ships off the Orkney Islands. Their leader explains that they, like Brutus, seek only a land in which to settle and ask Gurguit Barbtruc for a place to colonize. This king gives them no piece of Britain, but instead the entire island of Ireland, which is described in language, "omni vasta" (293) [all a wasteland], that echoes descriptions of early Britain. This story shows the British monarch to be generous, yet prudent. In his sympathy for the exiles, he helps them find a homeland.

The prose *Brut* tells nearly the same story about a British king named Corinbatrus. This version, however, heightens the Irish indebtedness to Britain and maintains that because of this encounter, Ireland is actually subject to Britain. These exiles seek: "eny kyng, or eny lorde, that of ham wolde haue pitee or mercy, toȝeue ham eny lande in eny contre wherin thai might duelle and haue reste, and bicome his liege men, and to him wolde done homage and feautes whiles that he leuede, and to his heires after him, and of him and of his heires holde that londe for euermore" (27). This text not only keeps foreign travelers at a distance from Britain, but also takes pains to make them subject to British political authority. The changes to this story emphasize the subordination of the foreign to the British rather than the obligation of a reciprocal alliance that exogamy would imply.

The *Brut* tells a similar story about the populating of Scotland. This narrative, however, makes marriage and the threat of foreign incursion a more explicit focus, setting the scene for the political strife among Scotland, Ireland, Britain, and France recounted in the second half of the *Brut*. This version preserves Geoffrey of Monmouth's narrative concerning the Picts, but transforms them into French invaders under King Rodrick. In both tales, when the invading army is defeated, the British king offers them an empty land where no one lives, Albany (Scotland.) Even though the Britons are willing to let foreigners live in Scotland, when the colonists ask them for British wives, they are refused.[9] While the Picts in Geoffrey's *Historia* had been described as wild barbarian fighters from Scythia, the French settlers under Berenger "biganne a toune, that thai myȝt therin duelle and haue resceyt...and bicome riche" (36). The British refusal to share brides with them exhibits the text's rejection of exogamy and refusal to mingle Britons and Scots both economically and genealogically.

This refusal, however, does not doom the Picts and the French to extinction, for in both texts they simply marry women from another group, the Irish, from the generation of the earlier exiles from Spain. The Britons keep foreign blood out of their race and foreign influence out of their country and politics. In their turn, however, the foreign settlers ally through marriage, and become politically united against British power. The rest of the British Isles become populated through marriage, and those generations harry British power in years to come. England's policy of refusing foreign marriage ties serves to create enemy states.

The British emphasis on endogamy can also be seen in its own colonizing efforts. Unlike the Scots and French, British colonists in Amorica (Brittany) will not marry local or foreign women, sending instead back to England for brides of British blood:

Conan Meriedok duellede in litel Britaigne with michel honour, and lete ordeyne ii M ploughmen of the lande forto erie the land, to harwe it and sowe, and feffede ham all rychely, after that thai were. and forasmiche that Kyng Conan, ne none of his kny3tes, ne none of his othere peple, wolde nou3t takes wifes of the nacion of Fraunce, he tho sent into grete Britaig[n]e, to the Erl of Cornewaile that me callede Dionotho, that chees throu3-oute alle the lande xi M of maydenes, that is to seyne, viii M for the mene peple, and iii M for the grettest lordes that schulde ham spouse. (43)

Conan's transport of Britons has two effects: it depopulates the island to such an extent that it becomes prey to foreign invasion, and the ships carrying the women never reach Amorica, instead becoming shipwrecked, with St. Ursula leading the women to vows of chastity and martyrdom. The immediate fate of the colonists in Amorica is not stated explicitly. Did they finally take local, French wives upon the loss of the British women? They do reproduce themselves, for in the next generation, the second son of the first British king in Amorica leads a force back to Britain to save it from foreign invasion. Although their British wives were denied them, the kings of Little Britain have regenerated a royal line that is so successful that it in turn recolonizes Britain (46). Their possible foreign marriages enable them to survive, while their British heritage creates a kinship tie that requires them to render aid to the homeland. These colonization efforts show Britain attempting to create an alliance without using exogamy with its attendant foreign and feminine presence.

In charting the various encounters between Britain and its neighboring people, the prose *Brut* explores how endogamy was often favored by the early Britons thus forgoing the alliances that political marriage could bring. This apprehension about the presence of foreigners in Britain attains a height with the beginning of Saxon incursions into the island. In the person of Ronewenne, the daughter of the Saxon Engist given to the British king Vortigern, the text most fully associates the feminine and the foreign, using this distrust of alien elements to reinforce its condemnation and suspicion of women who play prominent roles in national politics.

Vortigern is in a difficult position politically at the end of his story, for he has usurped the throne from his predecessor, and ordered him executed. He is unpopular with his nobles and the British people, and he even fears that Aurelius and Uther, the legitimate heirs, are massing an army to invade Britain. So when the Saxon forces of Engist and his brother, Horn, land in Kent seeking a new homeland, their fate is different from the earlier Irish and Scottish wanderers. Engist boasts to Vortigern that they are well-equipped colonists from Germany, chosen according to German custom to leave their overpopulated homeland because they were the "boldest that bene amonges ham and best mowen trauaile into diuerse3 londes" (50).[10] Unlike the earlier wanderers who seek a British overlord or British wives, the Saxons come as mercenary soldiers. Vortigern leaps at this opportunity to be freed from his political troubles, saying that "if thai my3t delyuer his lande of his enemys, he wolde 3eue ham resonable landes, wher thai shulde duelle for euermore" (51).

The Saxons, however, immediately prove their status as treacherous aliens by using a woman's trick. Like Dido before them, Engist proposes that the Saxons be granted only "as miche place as he my3t compasse with a twonge of a skyn" (51), which Vortigern easily grants. Engist of course cuts the skin into thin strips by which he encircles enough land upon which to build a city. Through feminine trickery, outsiders have gained a foothold in British territory.

Once the Saxons have been established as treacherous outsiders with designs on British territory, their foreign threat becomes even more feminized in the figure of Ronnewen, Engist's daughter. After the Saxon leader has built his castle, he opens the floodgates of immigration when he "priuely sent bi lettre into the contre that he come of, after an hundrede shippis fillede with strange men that were bolde and wel fei3tyng in alle batailes; and that thai shulde bryng with ham Ronewenne, his dou3ter, that was the fairest creature that eny man my3t see" (51). Along with a multitude of skilled warriors comes one beautiful woman; the text treats her as if she were her father's secret weapon, an embodiment of his trickery.

When Vortigern visits Engist's new stronghold, the Saxon leader sends Ronewenne to him to perform a seemingly innocent and ceremonial ritual of welcome: "when ny3t come, that the kyng shulde go into his chambre forto take there his ny3tes reste, Ronewenne...come with a coupe of golde in here honde, and knelede bifore the kyng, and saide to him 'Whatsaile!'" (52). Vortigern is dazzled and even confused by this Saxon ritual; he "saw the fairenesse of Ronewenne, and his armes layde aboute here nek, and thries swetely cussede hir and anone ry3t he was vnarmerede oppon hire, that he desirede to haue here to wyf" (52). This marriage is presented not as a judicious alliance, but as another trick perpetuated by Engist upon Vortigern and Britain, for Engist will agree to the marriage only upon the condition that he receive all of Kent for his people to live in. This union is described as "miche confusion" (52) for Vortigern, and immediately causes so much civil unrest that the British subjects reject their own king. Not only has Vortigern allowed a foreign tool of her Saxon father into his house, but because she is not a Christian ("he hade spousede a womman of mysbileue" [52]), his own people will not sanction the marriage.

In her initial appearance, Ronewenne is a cog in her father's plot to seduce British territory away from Vortigern. But as the wife of the British king, she becomes herself a treacherous foreign presence in the heart of the royal household. Unlike earlier queens whose marriages create strong alliances between husband and father, and who even negotiate peace between those two allegiances, Ronewenne does not transfer her primary loyalty to her husband or even begin to negotiate a difficult dual loyalty, as we see in the story of Vortimere.

Since Engist remains a dangerous force in England, the people choose Vortimere, Vortigern's son by his first wife to be their king and to drive the Saxons out of Kent. But even though Vortimere succeeds on the military front, because of Vortigern's marriage, the enemy remains within the domestic realm, within his own royal house. Ronewenne does not transfer her loyalties to her new British household, just as she has not become a Christian. After her father and the Saxons leave Britain, she remains and plots for their return, as she "made sorwe ynow, and queyntly spake to ham that were nexte the kyng Vortymere, and priueest with him. and so miche she ʒaf ham of ʒiftes, that he was apoysended, & deide at London the iii ʒere of his regne" (53). As a foreigner, Ronewenne remains an outsider and as a woman she grossly intervenes in the political processes of her adopted nation, poisoning the king chosen by the people, not merely to place her own husband back on his throne, but for the even greater danger of bringing her Saxon father back to British territory. Even though in this text, Vortigern has learned his lesson, Ronewenne, after her husband regains the crown, "sent priuely by letter to Engist that she hade enpoisended Vortymer...and that he shulde come aʒeyne into that lande, wel arraiede with miche peple, forto avenge him vppon the Britons, and to wynne his lande aʒeyne" (54). This exogamous marriage has brought foreign treachery in feminine form to the heart of British history: although Vortigern tries to fend off the Saxon forces, he is taken prisoner and the Britons must flee to Wales. And the name of Briton, which had held from the time of its founder Brutus, is changed to that of its new master—"Engistes lande" (55). Marriage politics give the people of Britain a new patronym and a new lineage displaces that of Brutus's generations.

Female figures in the prose *Brut* show increased tensions regarding their positions in narratives of succession and of political marriages. By locating Britain's origin in the tale of Albine and her sisters, and then supplanting it with the story of Brutus, the reformed parricide, this narration of Britain's past reveals an ambivalence regarding foreign and feminine presence in the island that resurfaces throughout the text. The final section of this chapter will examine how the contemporary poem *Sir Gawain and the Green Knight* situates the roles of female figures in a focused episode that tests King Arthur's court within the context of Trojan history expounded by late medieval chronicles such as the *Brut*.

Maternal Power and Generation in *Sir Gawain and the Green Knight*

Scholars have found the beginning of *Sir Gawain and the Green Knight* troublesome, with the historical premise seemingly unrelated to the well-crafted romance that follows. In perhaps the best treatment of the Trojan frame of the *Gawain*,[11] Alfred David argues that through this strategy, the poem tries to link the past and the present, that is, to connect the rise and fall of Troy with the testing of Arthur's tragic court. Although the correspondence between Troy and Britain does not reappear until the poem's final lines, "the Trojan allusions fit well into a pattern of rising and falling that constitute the very framework of the poem...when we have finished reading *Gawain*, we have gained a deeper insight into 'the Brutus bokes.'"[12] The conception of history expressed in the *Gawain*'s Trojan prologue, however, also goes beyond the cyclical pattern common in the Brut tradition. Beginning and ending with the matter of the legendary history of Troy and Britain as founded by Brutus, *Sir Gawain and the Green Knight* can be seen as a digressive, romance tale situated within the larger body of genealogical Brut histories popular at the time the poem was composed.

Sheila Fisher builds upon David's work on the Trojan frame, arguing that this cyclical emphasis signals clear connections in the poem between beginnings and endings. Fisher explicates the poem's gendered narrative by focusing on the revelation of Morgan Le Fay at the end of the poem. She argues that by pushing Morgan to the margin of the story, the poem is trying to remake its own history. Since women

are inextricably involved in narratives of the fall of civilizations—
Troy with Helen and Paris and the Arthurian court with Guenevere
and Lancelot—the text must "marginalize them in order to save its
story." But Fisher notes that this is impossible, for even if women are
legally and politically marginalized in medieval culture, "they are
central biologically, economically and politically to its continuation."[13] In essence, women are central to a conception of history as
progressive and successive and to the development of a narrative with
these qualities because they are generative figures.

Gayle Margherita begins to situate gender within the poem's consciousness of the historical discourse invoked by Britain's Trojan heritage. By comparing the generative role of Morgan to the way Juno
intervenes in the *Aeneid*, she posits that such female generated narratives interrupt and delay the imperial vision of history embodied in
Trojan tradition. In Margherita's eyes, Morgan represents a counter-
origin to the Trojan history that the poem openly acknowledges, and
the world that she creates—the landscape of Gawain's testing—
threatens the Arthur's imperial enterprise just as surely as Juno's establishment of Dido at Carthage undermines and delays Roman pretensions of a new Troy. She concludes that by situating the poem
within the generic context of epic, we can see how the "dilatory
pleasures of romance" throw into relief the "linear agenda of epic"[14]
and, I would argue, historical discourse more generally.

By delaying and impeding the epic enterprise cited in the *Gawain*'s opening lines, Morgan's romance echoes the function that
gender often plays in the prose *Brut*. Like Albine and her descendent
sisters such as Ronewenne, Morgan becomes an obstacle that inter-
rupts the narrative and betrays its communal purpose, to establish
and guarantee social order. Although Margherita's is a perceptive
analysis of the *Aeneid* and of how the *Gawain* poem may be equated
with romantic interludes within that epic, for the purposes of the late
medieval period in Europe, she overstates the linearity of epic and of
the "Brutes bookes" that *Sir Gawain and the Green Knight* invokes.
Digression is one of the defining characteristics of epic and is not always only a dilatory motion. Digressions, though often triggered by
feminine forces, allow a different way of engaging with the past,
showing it to be multifaceted, overlapping, incomplete, and break-
able, rather than fixed or successive or even conclusive. One need
only think of the numerous digressions in *Beowulf* that tell of its

hero's youth or of Nordic history. In both the *Aenied* and the *Odyssey*, the interludes begun by Dido, Venus, and Juno, or by Naussika and Athena, allow Aeneas and Odysseus to retell the history of Troy's fall and their subsequent wandering. These stories allow other versions of the past to co-exist with and complicate the linear pattern the dominant narrative seeks to establish.

While Morgan's test of Arthur's court creates a digression from the patterns of British history, her engineering of the narrative, as well as the portraits of other female figures, is far from the "afterthought" that Margherita describes.[15] The analysis of the prose *Brut* above has illustrated that even at this late date, medieval British conceptions of the past used a complex relationship among female figures, reproduction, and the production of history; women sometimes perform transgressive acts and at other times authoritative and legitimating ones, in order to direct or diffuse tensions in succession, marriage practices, and their political contexts. Morgan's role, coupled with the positioning of Mary, Guenevere, and the Lady, partakes of this tension between linguistic and sexual transgression and a kind of legitimating, reproductive authority that women possess in historiographic tradition.

Gawain's much discussed anti-feminist diatribe near the end of the poem[16] represents well the tensions among the figurings of women, reproduction, and history by implying that transgressive women cannot reproduce a satisfactory new generation. The form of the diatribe is nearly genealogical, starting as most genealogies do with Adam, and it allows Gawain to put himself in the direct line of Samson, Soloman and King David as men who had been betrayed by the wiles of women. As Gawain exclaims:

"I haf soiorned sadly; sele yow bytyde,
And he 3elde hit you 3are that 3arkkez al menskes!
And comaundez me to that cortays, your comlych fere,
Bothe that on and that other, myn honoured ladyez,
That thus hor kny3t with hor kest han koyntly bigyled.
Bot hit is no ferly tha3 a fole madde,
And thur3 wyles of wymmen be wonen to sor3e,
For so watz Adam in erde with one bygyled,
And Salamon with fele sere, and Samson eftsonez—
Dalyda dalt hym hys wyrde—and Dauyth therafter
Watz blended with Barsabe, that much bale tholed.
Now these were wrathed with her wyles, hit were a wynne huge
To luf hom wel, and leue hem not, a leude that couthe.
For thes wer forne the freest, that fol3ed alle the sele

Exellently of alle thyse other, vnder heuenryche that mused;
And alle thay were biwyled
With wymmen that thay vsed.
Thaȝ I be now Bigyled,
Me think me burde be excused." (2411–2428)[17]

Bertilak's lady and the Crone, Morgan, also take their place in this generation of history for they are called descendants of Eve, Delilah, and Bathsheba, women who inhabit the transgressive tradition estab-lihed in the *Brut* chronicle by Albine and her various sisters. Al-though the men invoked in Gawain's speech are Biblical patriarchs, because the women who are included are so wily, they produce tricky words rather than children that could provide a stable transition to the future. Eve through her sin becomes a problematic origin for the generations of man. Bathsheba particularly marks the failure of mar-riage systems of exchange, for David sends her husband Uriah to cer-tain death in order to possess his wife. The women and men described by Gawain become signs of verbal and corporeal excess, rather than contained figures that reproduce within the regulated genealogical schema of history.

This lineage of tricked men and treacherous women points to the problem of production at the heart of the Arthurian schema—as Peggy McCracken has shown, adulterous women are usually and somewhat inexplicably barren, with sexual transgression becoming the way the text figures them rhetorically, rather than the authority of mother-hood and queenship that narratives of succession and reproduction can give aristocratic women.[18] While Arthur's court promises future "blisse," his queen is barren and adulterous; the only new generation the story produces is an incestuous and treacherous one, that of Mordred. In the end, this genealogy of treacherous women and be-trayed men does produce an heir to carry on its tradition. With women styled only as treacherous, Gawain's history can only beget more of the same. And with Guenevere tacitly invoked by Gawain's list of treacherous women, it is not he who should take his place as the heir to Adam, Samson, and David, but Arthur.[19]

The maternal, however, as in the *Brut* chronicle, remains an im-portant, if residual source of authority in the poem and still brings legitimacy in complex ways to its action and the construction of its female figures. Gawain is Mary's knight with her image, of course, on the inside of his shield, opposite the pentangle, one point of which symbolizes her sorrow at the death of her son.[20] The central presence of the Christian, Virgin Mother allows other figures to partake in the contradictory authority, based on the reproducing body, that maternal figures can and do offer to their own actions and to those they sponsor. For instance, in the moment of Gawain's vindication, just after the Green Knight nicks his neck with the ax, Gawain's "rebirth" is told in terms of his original birth:

> And quen the burne seȝ the blode blenk on the snawe,
> He sprit forth spenne-fote more then a spere lenth,
> Hent heterly his helme, and on his hed cast,
> Schot with his schulderez his fayre schelde vnder,
> Braydez out a bryȝt sworde, and bremely he spekz—
> Neuer syn that he watz burne of his moder
> Watz he neuer in this worlde wyȝe half so blythe—(2315–2321)

Invoking birth imagery legitimates this moment and Gawain's new life.

Scholars have argued that female figures in the poem serve as stand-ins for one another.[21] Mary, in her maternal, reproductive guise, is conflated with Morgan. When Gawain prays to Mary for Christmas shelter, and a place to attend mass, he receives Morgan, the Lady, and Bertilak's castle in answer to his petition. Morgan remains associated with fertility, although the text portrays her as treacherous. She uses maternal-like authority to ground her testing of Gawain. Often confused with her sister, Morgause, as the mother of Mordred (which makes her Gawain's aunt) Morgan, in this sense is "the Goddess," like Mary, God's mother, and so is capable of generating a text that will test the court, and "to haf greued Gaynour and gart hir to dyȝe" (2460)—exposing the barren core that tradition places at the heart of Arthur's court.

At the turn of the fifteenth century, stories of the legendary British past remained popular with aristocratic readers across England. Seemingly disregarding generic distinctions that modern critics make between chronicle and romance tales, narratives in both genres tell similar tales and betray similar political emphases. By examining *Sir Gawain and the Green Knight* within the context of the kind of "Brutus bookes" it invokes, this analysis reveals that the poem's treatment of Morgan and other female figures may have been informed by conjunctions that can be found between narratives of genealogical succession and of political marriages that insert foreign women in English lineages in the late versions of the chronicle tradition. This tradition, first articulated by Geoffrey of Monmouth in his *Historia regum Britanniae*, deploys female figures in various, often contradictory positions from which they could legitimate, but also confound the politics of reproduction and the production of narrative. At these moments, both chronicles and romances partake of one another's rhetorical strategies—although Morgan stands condemned by Gawain as an otherworldly figure in a lineage of treacherous women who will confound the future bliss of the Arthurian court, she partakes in the kind of textual authority that genealogical chronicles grant reproducing women, that of legitimating the national narrative.

CONCLUSION

t the beginning of *Persuasion*, Jane Austen describes how the vain Sir Walter Elliot customarily reads over his own genealogy in the British peerage:

> there he found occupation for an idle hour and consolation in a distressed one; there his faculties were roused into admiration and respect...there any unwelcome sensations arising from domestic affairs, changed...as he turned over the almost endless creations of the last century—and there, if every other leaf were powerless, he could read his own history with an interest which never failed.[1]

Sir Walter's genealogy lists his own birth, his marriage, and the births of his children. He, himself, has written in subsequent events such as the death of his wife, the marriage of his youngest daughter, and the name of his nephew, the family heir. Although he does not admit it, the continuity of this history of the years of his family is in some jeopardy. As the novel explains, Miss Elliot, Sir Walter's eldest daughter, so like her father in temperament and interests, no longer enjoyed reading the family history for "always to be presented with the date of her own birth, and see no marriage follow...made the book an evil; and more than once...had she closed it, with averted eyes, and pushed it away."[2]

Persuasion, of course, like most of Austen's works, takes the "marriage plot," the social and economic workings of this institution, as its subject. Although far removed in many ways from the English chronicles and romances studied here, the novel astutely joins the concerns of history, familial succession, and property, with the workings of marriage, and social and sexual regulation. A strong succession would have brought peace of mind to Sir Walter and economic security to his daughters, but the tricky management of the marriages that are needed to provide the future of the lineage becomes the conflict for the novel to resolve. *Persuasion*'s opening scene reveals the personal stake even later British readers placed upon their lineages and on the formation of the marriages that created them.

While the aristocratic audiences of late medieval England are not the country gentry of Austen's novel, the concerns of creating lineage and preserving the succession of property also permeated their textual and political worlds. By examining selected aspects of the reception of Geoffrey of Monmouth's genealogical history of Britain in both the traditions of the romance and popular chronicle, this study has argued that the gendered politics of dynastic succession occupies a pivotal rhetorical position in these works where the genres of chronicle and romance intersect, where the sequential narration of genealogy and the plots of marriage intertwine, and where coordinate paratactic style breaks into subordinate digressions and conflicts. The contingent nature of the past and the difficulty and social tensions involved in reproducing it become more evident at these textual junctures. At these points, therefore, the texts foreground outcast figures like Brut, but more often focus on polysemous female figures through which they can attempt to resolve challenges to the paternal schema of lineage and return to the smooth passage of years. In this way, texts could use or even appropriate the cultural authority vested in the maternal function of these figures to legitimate the origins and continuity of the past. In addition to producing children, however, these figures could produce speech, and in both these functions could transgress and subvert the paternal aims of genealogy, breaking the succession rather than preserving it. As such potentially threatening figures, women in these historical texts often drew tensions surrounding ethnic and linguistic difference. While recognizing the valences that tradition has vested in female figures, however, this study strives to situate these figures and historical women within specific textual and cultural contexts.[3]

Geoffrey of Monmouth uses this complex dynamic to point out the constructed and fragile nature of the lineages he traces for the British kings. His awareness of himself as a writer of history allows him a freedom with his material that subsequent historians have condemned, but also gives his *Historia* a generic and stylistic complexity that other participants in medieval textual communities through the years would seize upon to create a vital tradition of Vergilian and Arthurian narrative that would cross generic and linguistic boundaries.

By collaborating on the composition of the Anglo-Norman *Les Croni-cles*, Nicholas Trevet and his patron Mary of Woodstock were able to explore and preserve women's often contradictory, yet important presence on the historical stage. As a reader of this tradition, Chaucer responds in his *Man of Law's Tale* with a narrative that explores the reduced role that passivity and distance from her maternal role can bring to a royal woman such as Constance. As a late version of Geof-frey's history, the *Brut* chronicle responds to his tradition by empha-sizing female figures' disruptive and transgressive origins in the tale of Albine and her sisters and most clearly ties anxieties surrounding these figures to misgivings about foreign marriages of the elite. The contemporary romance, *Sir Gawain and the Green Knight*, however, explicitly ties its action to a genealogical framework of Trojan history and uses the reproductive and transgressive properties of Morgan le Fay to critique Gawain's chivalry and the future of Arthur and Guenevere's court.

The readers and authors who participated in the production of these texts, like Geoffrey of Monmouth, exploited the intersections between narratives of genealogy and the progression of time, and the narratives of marriage and romance which with difficulty, allow the reproduction of lineage and history. By exploring gender in this rhe-torical context, this study argues that historical narratives, as well as some authors and readers, use the genres of chronicle and romance to resist and perhaps revise the constraints that familial politics, with its accompanying gender roles, could impose upon them. For, to return to a later reader, Anne Elliot, unlike her elder sister, does not push her history away, but in the course of Austen's novel, uses the limited means at her disposal to revise the earlier marriage narrative that her relations and their interests had forced upon her.

NOTES

Introduction: Medieval Genres: Combining the Study of Historiography and Romance

1. Susan Crane, *Insular Romance: Politics, Faith, and Culture in Anglo-Norman and Middle English Literature* (Berkeley: University of California Press, 1986), 15.

2. Robert W. Hanning, *The Individual in Twelfth-Century Romance* (New Haven: Yale University Press, 1977), 60.

3. Roberta L. Krueger, *Women Readers and the Ideology of Gender in Old French Verse Romance* (Cambridge: Cambridge University Press, 1993), 1–3.

4. Simon Gaunt argues that masculinity and femininity are figured in different, but closely related ways in the French traditions of chanson de geste and romance. While women are frequently present in the chanson, they are excluded from the poems' value system. Gaunt maintains that this strategy allows masculinity to be constructed, not in simple opposition to femininity, but "in relation to other models of masculinity" creating gender "as a problematic process whose success and failures as a system leave it open to question" (22–23). Romances also "represent women as other to further create male subjectivity" (72), but while the chansons do not put women in central kinship or hierarchical structures, the romances do. See his *Gender and and Genre in Medieval French Literature* (Cambridge: Cambridge University Press, 1995). On women readers, see Krueger, *Women Readers*, 17–24.

5. Walter J. Ong, *Orality and Literacy: The Technologizing of the Word* (London: Methuen & Co, 1982). Scholars have also looked for this progression within the genres of medieval history and romance. For instance, Cecily Clark finds a developing sophistication in the style of the *Anglo-Saxon Chronicle* that parallels the politicization of its various versions, responding to the troubled times of William the Conqueror and his contesting heirs. See her "The Narrative Mode of the *Anglo-Saxon Chronicle* before the Conquest," in *England before the Conquest: Studies in Honor of Dorothy Whitelock*, ed. Peter Clemoes and Katherine Hughes (Cambridge: Cambridge University Press, 1971), 234. Scholars have also used the opposition between parataxis and hypotaxis, with its accompanying values of orality and literacy, to categorize different types of medieval history—the annal, chronicle, and

history—equating the amount of subordination in each type with the degree of sophistication and "objective" historical analysis.

6. Brian Stock, *The Implications of Literacy: Written Language and Models of Interpretation in the Eleventh and Twelfth Centuries* (Princeton: Princeton University Press, 1983). Also see: Daniel Donoghue and Bruce Mitchell, "Parataxis and Hypotaxis: A Review of Some Terms Used for Old English Syntax" *Neuphilologische Mitteilungen* 93.2 (1992): 163–83; Andreas H. Jucker, "Between Hypotaxis and Parataxis: Clauses of Reason in *Ancrene Wisse*," in *Historical English Syntax*, ed. Dieter Kastovsky (Berlin: Mouton de Gruyter, 1991), 203–20; Valerie Krishna, "Parataxis, Formulaic Density, and Thrift in the *Alliterative Morte Arthure*," *Speculum* 57.1 (1982): 63–83.

7. Joan Wallach Scott offers several ways to understand how gender functions in narratives as politically motivated as these late medieval chronicles and romances. Scott first asserts that narrative is in itself gendered, and as such can be used as a means of legitimizing a social or intellectual agenda because "conceptual languages employ differentiation to establish meaning, and sexual differentiation is a primary way of signifying differentiation" (45). Law and civil society are created through differentiation, through distinguishing the allowable from the taboo and the insider from the outsider. The conception of gender opposition in a text can be tied to these pivotal cultural oppositions. Thus gender becomes one of the "recurrent references by which political power has been conceived, legitimated, and criticized....to vindicate political power, the reference must seem sure and fixed, outside human construction, part of the natural or divine order. In this way, the binary opposition and social process of gender relationships both become part of the meaning of power itself" (49). See her *Gender and the Politics of History* (New York: Columbia University Press, 1988).

8. Hayden White, "The Value of Narrativity in the Representation of Reality," in *The Content of the Form: Narrative Discourse and Historical Representation* (Baltimore: Johns Hopkins University Press, 1987), 11.

9. Scholars of romance suggest that the gaps in paratactic medieval texts are recognized by their readers and that these actively participate in creating the meaning of the narrative. For instance, Erich Auerbach, in a study of the episode in the *Chanson de Roland* in which Ganelon succeeds in convincing Charlemagne to give the dangerous command of the rearguard to Roland, describes the representational technique of the chanson as "string[ing] independent pictures together like beads" (115). Between these pictures are "intervals" which allow each element to be taken out of its immediate historical and literary context and to be set in juxtaposition to one another. To Auerbach, each scene then nearly achieves the symbolic and moral authority of an *exemplum*. Although he does not acknowledge that he is privileging readerly activity in his analysis, his interpretation provides an example of his theory of *figural* reading or thought. See Erich Auerbach, *Mimesis: The Representation of Reality in Western Literature*, trans. Willard R. Trask (Princeton: Princeton University Press, 1968).

More recent critics also explore the role of the reader in the creation of this kind of text. John P. Boots argues that the juxtaposition of events "quali-fie[s], reinforce[s], complement[s] and otherwise comment[s] on one another" (4) and that "trained contemporary readers can see the parallels, and con-trasts"(4) and gauge the meaning of the text. The message wrought by para-taxis is a subtly political one, a thesis that Boots claims can overcome many critical expectations that romance is an "extrahistorical genre" (6–7). See his "Parataxis and Politics: Meaning and the Social Utility of Middle English Romances," in *A Humanist's Legacy: Essays in Honor of John Christian Bale*, ed. Dennis M. Jones (Decorah, IA: Luther College, 1990), 3–10. Bonnie Wheeler and Jo Goyne take a more performative stance on how the reader participates in the making of the text. For Wheeler, the gaps in Malory's text create an ambiguous narrative. Like the figures in the test narrative, who must choose responsible action, readers must seek their own way through the textual web, making their own associations and putting together the pat-terns that Malory never makes explicit. Goyne takes Wheeler's work a step farther, arguing that "the omissions created by Malory's style tease the reader with possibilities, actively involving one in the experience of composing the tale...to fill in those gaps herself" (38). See Bonnie Wheeler, "Romance and Parataxis and Malory," *Arthurian Literature* 13 (1993): 109–32, and Jo Goyne, "Parataxis and Causality in the Tale of Sir Launcelot Du Lake," *Quondam et Futurus: A Journal of Arthurian Interpretations* 2.4 (Winter 1992): 38–48.

10. Gabrielle Speigel, "Genealogy: Form and Function in Medieval Historical Narrative," *History and Theory* 22 (1983): 52.

11. White, "Value of Narrativity," 14.

12. For an explanation of this term, see Gayle Rubin, "The Traffic in Women," in *Toward an Anthropology of Women*, ed. Rayna R. Reiter (New York: Monthly Press Review, 1975), 157–210.

13. For a general overview of these issues, see R. Howard Bloch, *Etymologies and Genealogies: A Literary Anthropology of the French Middle Ages* (Chicago: University of Chicago Press, 1983).

14. Georges Duby, *The Chivalrous Society*, trans. Cynthia Postan (Berkeley: University of California Press, 1977), 153–57; Georges Duby, *The Knight, the Lady, and the Priest: The Making of Modern Marriage in Medieval France*, trans. Barbara Bray (New York: Pantheon Books, 1983), 92–95.

15. David Herlihy, *Medieval Households* (Cambridge, MA: Harvard University Press, 1985), 83.

16. Bryce Lyon, *A Constitutional and Legal History of Medieval England* (New York: Harper and Row, 1960), 138–39.

17. Crane, *Insular Romance*, 7–8, 14.

18. Speigel, "Genealogy," 48.

19. In her work on the mythic genealogies produced by the ancient Greek writer, Hesiod, Anne L. T. Bergren has found that sexual reproduction grounds fe-male figures' ability to produce signs—because they produce children, they alone can speak either truly or falsely to the legitimacy of this next genera-tion. In order to naturalize patriarchal succession, genealogies usurp this re-

productive, female authority by suppressing female figures, or in the case of many Greek gods, literally eating the mothers and producing children from their own bodies. See her "Language and the Female in Early Greek Thought," *Arethusa* 16 (1983): 69–95. See also Margaret Homans, "Feminist Criticism and Theory: The Ghost of Creusa," *Yale Journal of Criticism* 1 (1987–88): 153–82.

20. In a critique of Caroline Walker Bynum's *Holy Feast and Holy Fast: The Religious Significance of Food to Medieval Women* (Berkeley: University of California Press, 1987), Kathleen Biddick cautions that we resist an ahistorical reduction of the feminine to the maternal, that is, grounding our conceptions of gender in essentialized notions of the body, rather than in cultural processes. See Kathleen Biddick, "Genders, Bodies, Borders: Technologies of the Visible," *Speculum* 68 (1993): 389–418. For more information on motherhood in the Middle Ages, see Clarissa W. Atkinson, *The Oldest Vocation: Christian Motherhood in the Middle Ages* (Ithaca: Cornell University Press, 1991).

21. Peggy McCracken, "The Body Politic and the Queen's Adulterous Body in French Romance," in *Feminist Approaches to the Body in Medieval Literature*, ed. Linda Lomperis and Sarah Stanbury (Philadelphia: University of Pennsylvania Press, 1993), 38–64.

Chapter One: Gender, Genealogy, and the Politics of Succession in Geoffrey of Monmouth's *Historia regum Britanniae*

1. Not much is known about Geoffrey of Monmouth. He refers to himself in his writing as *Galfridus Monemutensis*, leading scholars to conclude Monmouth, near Wales, to be his birthplace. Thorpe writes that surviving biographical details prove him to have been Welsh, or at least a Breton living in Wales. From 1129–1151, he was connected with the town of Oxford and some suggest he may have been a canon there; see Lewis Thorpe, trans., *History of the Kings of Britain by Geoffrey of Monmouth* (London: Penguin Books, 1966), 13–14. It was at Oxford, in about 1138, that Geoffrey wrote the *Historia regum Britanniae*.

2. Antonia Gransden, *Historical Writing in England, c. 550-c. 1307* (Ithaca: Cornell University Press, 1974), 202–03. In contrast see the recent study by Patricia Clare Ingham, *Sovereign Fantasies: Arthurian Romance and the Making of Britain* (Philadelphia: University of Pennsylvania Press, 2001), which argues that "accounts of early British history that pit the excesses of Monmouth's extravagant fiction against other more sober truths implicitly encode fears about the popularity and the cultural powers of his text" (22). For more on Geoffrey as historian see also Christopher Brooke, "Geoffrey of Monmouth as a Historian," in *Church and Government in the Middle Ages*, ed. Christopher Brooke, D. Luscombe, G. Martin, and D. Owen (Cambridge: Cambridge University Press: 1976), 77–91. On legendary history more generally, see Nancy F. Partner, *Serious Entertainments: The Writing of History in Twelfth-Century England* (Chicago: University of Chicago Press, 1977).

3. This account of Britain's past was extremely popular in its day. About two hundred copies survive, a large number for a medieval text. Fifty or so date from the twelfth century and the manuscript continued to be copied throughout the fifteenth century. See Acton Griscom, ed., *The Historia Regum Britanniae of Geoffrey of Monmouth*, (London: Longmans, Green and Co., 1929; reprint Geneva: Slatkine Reprints, 1977), 19, 573–77. Lister M. Matheson urges us to recognize that the *Historia regum Britanniae* was a "living text," with its own existence through the period, influencing historical narratives as well as literary culture. See his "King Arthur and the Medieval English Chronicles," in *King Arthur Through the Ages*, ed. Valerie M. Lagorio and Mildred Leake Day (New York: Garland, 1990), 1.249.

Many histories and chronicles through the Middle Ages derive from the *Historia regum Britanniae* or incorporate its text within their own. John Taylor lists many such *Brut* chronicles in French through the fourteenth century when they began to circulate in English as the anonymous prose *Brut*; John Taylor, *English Historical Literature in the Fourteenth Century* (Oxford: Clarendon Press, 1987), 110. Nicholas Trevet's *Les Cronicles* and Ranulf Higden's *Polychronicon*, among other texts, use it as their primary source for early British history. Versions of the *Historia* were passed on to Renaissance culture when *Polychronicon* and the *Brut* were printed by Caxton. Through the *Brut* tradition, Geoffrey of Monmouth's text becomes incorporated in Holinshed's history, an important source for Shakespeare's history plays.

Literary texts also derive from the *Historia regum Britanniae*. Geoffrey Gaimar adapted it to Old French in the 1140s, and his version was replaced in the manuscripts by another early revision, the *Roman de Brut*, an 1155 paraphrase of the *Historia regum Britanniae* into Anglo-Norman by Wace. Wace was translated into Middle English by Layamon in the early thirteenth century as his *Brut*, but this version had little subsequent literary influence. Wace's *Roman de Brut*, however, gives the material of Geoffrey's history to the French romance writers, and by the early thirteenth century, the vulgate Arthurian cycles hold a firm place in French literary culture. These versions form the source for Thomas Malory's fifteenth-century translations, *Morte D'Arthure*.

Critics such as M. Victoria Guerin continue to work with sources; see her "The King's Sin: the Origins of the David-Arthur Parallel," in *The Passing of Arthur: New Essays in Arthurian Tradition*, ed., Christopher Baswell and William Sharpe (New York: Garland, 1988), 15–30. Critics such as Nancy Vine Durling and Lister M. Matheson trace the rich influence Geoffrey's text had upon subsequent French and English romances and histories. See Nancy Vine Durling, "Translation and Innovation in the *Roman de Brut*," in *Medieval Translators and Their Craft*, ed. Jeanette Beer, *Studies in Medieval Culture* 25 Medieval Institute Publications (Kalamazoo, MI: Western Michigan University Press, 1989), 9–40; Matheson, "King Arthur," 248–74.

4. Maureen Fries explores Boethian themes, arguing that the text shows that faulty self-rule exiles the individual, the king, and the nation from their true home, and Susan M. Shwartz argues against Robert Hanning by saying that the *Historia regum Britanniae* is still sacred history because its pattern of founding, betrayal, and diaspora is based on New and Old Testament models.

See Maureen Fries, "Boethian Themes and Tragic Structure in Geoffrey of Monmouth's *Historia Regum Britanniae*," in *The Arthurian Tradition: Essays in Convergence*, ed. Mary Flowers Braswell and John Bugge (Tuscaloosa: University of Alabama Press, 1988), 29–42; Susan M. Shwartz, "The Founding and Self-Betrayal of Britain: An Augustinian Approach to Geoffrey of Monmouth's *Historia Regum Britanniae*," *Medievalia et Humanistica: Studies in Medieval and Renaissance Culture*, ns 10 (1981), 33–54. For Robert Hanning's seminal work on Geoffrey of Monmouth, see his *The Vision of History in Early Britain from Gildas to Geoffrey of Monmouth* (New York: Columbia University Press, 1966).

5. See Lee Patterson, "The Romance of History and the Alliterative *Morte Arthure*," in *Negotiating the Past: The Historical Understanding of Medieval Literature* (Madison, WI: University of Wisconsin Press, 1987), 197–230. Richard Waswo writes more generally of the political use of origin myths in his "The History that Literature Makes," *New Literary History* 19.3 (Spring 1988): 541–64 and his "Our Ancestors, the Trojans: Inventing Cultural Identity in the Middle Ages," *Exemplaria* 7.2 (Fall 1995): 269–90. Stephen Knight emphasizes a different aspect of the political environment, arguing that the *Historia* not only justified the Norman conquest, but also explored contemporary political anxieties by echoing political figures (e.g. Cordelia as Henry I) and probing issues such as the problem of inheritance. The text became for its Norman audiences a sort of wish fulfillment, safely exploring political problems. See Knight, "'So Great a King': Geoffrey of Monmouth's *Historia Regum Britannia*," in *Arthurian Literature and Society* (London: Macmillan, 1983), 38–67. Jean Blacker, however, maintains that Geoffrey's purposes are nationalistic and show that even though their Trojan heritage legitimated British rule, they lost that rule because they fought among themselves; this is a lesson to the contemporary Norman kings. See Jean Blacker, "Transformations of a Theme: The Depoliticization of the Arthurian World in the *Roman de Brut*," in *The Arthurian Tradition: Essays in Convergence* ed. Mary Flowers Braswell and John Bugge (Birmingham: University of Alabama Press, 1988), 54–74; also see Jean Blacker, *The Faces of Time: Portrayal of the Past in Old French and Latin Historical Narrative of the Anglo-Norman Regnum* (Austin: University of Texas Press, 1994). Fiona Tolhurst has recently argued that Geoffrey's use of Biblical and Roman stories supports Matilda's claim to the British throne. See Fiona Tolhurst, "The Britons as Hebrews, Normans, and Romans: Geoffrey of Monmouth's British Epic and Reflections of Empress Matilda," *Arthuriana* 8.4 (1998): 69–87.

6. See: Francis Ingledew, "The Book of Troy and the Genealogical Construction of History: The Case of Geoffrey of Monmouth's *Historia regum Britanniae*," *Speculum* 69.3 (July 1994): 665–704, which characterizes the *Historia regum Britanniae* as a Vergilian narrative that encodes genealogy, prophecy, and *eros* within its imperial design; Michelle R. Warren, *History on the Edge: Excalibur and the Borders of Britain, 1100–1300* (Minneapolis: University of Minnesota Press, 2000), which argues that the *Historia* represents an ambivalent colonial fantasy; a special edition of *Arthuriana* 8.4 (Winter 1998) edited

by Fiona Tolhurst, which surveys current theoretical approaches to Geoffrey's work; Geraldine Heng, "Cannibalism, the First Crusade, and the Genesis of Medieval Romance," *Differences: A Journal of Feminist Cultural Studies* 10.1 (Spring 1998): 98–174, which argues that the romance tales in the *Historia* negotiate the social and political traumas of recent Anglo-Norman history through the development of a narrative of fantasy.

7. For two exceptions see Hanning, *Vision of History*, which argues that Geoffrey shaped his material in a new way by finding cycles and patterns in the chronological repetition of his sources, a method that resulted in the first secular vision of Britain's past, illustrating its tragic, and recurrent, rise and fall, and Valerie I. J. Flint, who has asserted that Geoffrey's Latin boldly parodies the historical writing of his day, subtly defending secular society and creating an alternative to clerical culture. See Flint, "The *Historia regum Britanniae* of Geoffrey of Monmouth: Parody and its Purpose: A Suggestion," *Speculum* 54.3 (July 1979): 447–68.

8. It is difficult to determine whether Geoffrey's decidedly secular history had aristocratic patronage. In the early twelfth century, the mechanisms of patronage that became so prominent with the later court of Henry II and Eleanor of Aquitaine had only begun to develop, and Henry I and Stephen were not well known as patrons; see Blacker, *Faces of Time*, 136. Geoffrey did dedicate his text to at least three powerful nobles. The earliest manuscripts show a double dedication to Robert of Gloucester, the illegitimate son of Henry I who fought against Stephen to put his half-sister Matilda on the British throne, and to Waleran of Beaumont, who had been close to Henry I, but later supported Stephen's claims to the throne. A single manuscript, however, copied soon after the earliest, substitutes Stephen's name in the first paragraph as the primary dedicatee, and puts Robert into the second paragraph, leaving out Waleran. One other manuscript is dedicated only to Robert and later editions include no dedication at all; see Griscom, *Historia regum Britanniae*, 43. Blacker argues that although Robert of Gloucester was undoubtedly the primary dedicatee of the history, Geoffrey, with his double dedications, was trying to appeal to and curry favor with the leaders of opposing factions in the succession struggles which followed the death of Henry I; see *Faces of Time*, 162–63.

Geoffrey wrote this history of British kings in a decidedly charged political atmosphere. As Stephen Knight writes, "the Normans' competitive search for property and glory" is emplotted by the internecine strife of Geoffrey's early kings and the difficulty of female succession is also an implicit issue. He concludes that these concerns are not overt, but through repeated narrative emphasis of contemporary concerns, the text became for its Norman audiences a sort of wish fulfillment, by which they could safely explore political problems. See Knight, "So Great a King," 47. Another recent critic, Valerie Flint suggests that Geoffrey's purpose was to exalt "responsible rulership and marriage," through portraying the "physical bravery of men, the judicious influence of women, and the power for good in society of family care and pride," an emphasis that not only provided a lesson to aristocrats, but also rebuked the celibate life increasingly urged by monastic movements. See Flint, *Historia regum Britanniae*, 463.

9. These years were rather chaotic ones for the dynasty of Norman kings: it had been only seventy years since William took the British throne and there had been only three Norman kings of England. Saxon and even Danish claimants still pressed. The first Norman kings had already been beset with conflicts over the secession. Primogeniture had not yet been accepted as the rule, and both William Rufus and Henry I had had to hold off the challenges of their older brother, Robert Curthose of Normandy. Assumptions of male rule were also challenged when Henry swore his nobles to support the claims of his daughter Matilda, the former Holy Roman Empress, after the death of his only legitimate son, William.

10. Patterson, "Romance of History." 199.

11. Speigel, "Genealogy," 48–50.

12. Teresa De Lauretis, "Desire in Narrative," in *Alice Doesn't: Feminism, Semiotics, Cinema* (Bloomington, IN: Indiana University Press, 1984), 103–57.

13. Marjorie Chibnall, *The Empress Matilda: Queen Consort, Queen Mother, and Lady of the English* (Oxford: Blackwell, 1991), 64.

14. The plot of romance can vary in its particulars and in its emphases according to its specific cultural milieu, but some of its characteristics are constants. The hero becomes alienated in some way from his culture, enters into a quest or test, and upon its successful completion, is re-integrated into the community. See Hanning, *Vision of History*, 214 n. 52. Hanning characterizes this narrative as centering upon the individual hero's identity and destiny, saying "the romance plot lacks any context larger than the lives of its protagonists" (*Individual in Twelfth-Century Romance*, 60) and without such a context, can function to explore metaphorically both chivalric values and how an individual knight creates himself in response to and in accordance with that system.

15. See the discussion of the work of Hayden White and Lee Patterson in the Introduction above.

16. For instance, Teresa De Lauretis describes the archetypal romance plot according to structuralist and folkloric paradigms, but her analysis emphasizes as well an awareness of the gendered aspects of how figures progress through the standard plot. The hero is displaced; he must go on a journey and overcome obstacles; a woman awaits him at the end of the story to reward his struggle; their union provides narrative closure and social affirmation. For De Lauretis, the narrative process is explicitly a gendered one for the active space of the hero is gendered masculine, while the plot spaces of the obstacle and the reward are feminine. Each of these narrative roles generates specific models for gendered behavior that have differing impacts on the processes by which readers view them. Men identify with the hero, and women identify not only with the female spaces, but also the positive and actively heroic male. De Lauretis characterizes this process as a complex, double identifica-

tion on the part of women with both aspects of the plot. See "Desire in Narrative," 121.

17. Gaunt, *Gender and Genre*, 1–3.

18. Latin quotations of Geoffrey's text are taken from Griscom. English translations are based on Thorpe; those uncited are my own. Other useful editions are: Edmond Faral , ed., *Historia regum Britanniae*, in *La Legende arthurienne—Etdues and documents*. 3 vols. (Paris: Champion, 1929); Jacob Hammer, ed., *The Historia Regum Britanniae of Geoffrey of Monmouth: A Varient Version*, Publications of the Medieval Academy of America. 57. (Cambridge, MA: Medieval Academy of America, 1951); Neil Wright, ed., *The Historia Regum Britanniae of Geoffrey of Monmouth I: Bern, Burgerbibliothetk, MS 568: II The First Varient Version, A Critical Edition* (Cambridge: D. S. Brewer, 1984; 1988). A useful commentary is provided by J. S. P. Tatlock, *The Legendary History of Britain: Geoffrey of Monmouth's "Historia Regum Britaniae" and its Early Vernacular Versions* (Berkeley: University of California Press, 1950; reprint New York: Gordian Press, 1974).

19. See Hanning, *The Vision of History*, 134–38, for this sequence of adaptation. Hanning argues that it is by going back beyond the providential "fall of Britain" tropes elaborated by Bede and Gildas to the British "pre-history" first written by the Nennius compilation, that Geoffrey is able to write the first "secular" pattern for British history.

20. Livy, *The Early History of Rome*, trans. Aubrey de Selincourt (New York: Penguin Books, 1960), 34–101. Livy, however, stresses continuity and unity for the people under Aeneas' control, saying that the Latins and Trojans were becoming one people and that the Latins were as loyal to Aeneas as the Trojans because he had renamed all his followers Latins, losing his name in accordance with Dido's curse at the end of *Aeneid* 4.

21. Cf. the conclusion of *Aenied* 2 in which Aeneas' wife, Creusa, is expediently eliminated to be replaced by the Latin Lavinia. Margaret Homans comments on this removal of the mother in the epic quest narrative and "her replacement...by a wife whose lesser powers make her more readily serve patrilineal needs." Homans, "Feminist Criticism and Theory," 157.

22. See Rubin, "Traffic in Women," for a feminist overview of anthropological studies of these phenomena.

23. That Silvius's illicit affair with Lavinia's niece is a critical juncture for lineage and imperial pretensions is confirmed by the way Geoffrey echoes Virgil in this passage. In *Aeneid* 4, Dido and Aeneas' meeting in the cave during a violent storm sent by Juno is described as a "furtivum amorem" (4.171) or "secret love" as glossed by Austin. Virgil calls this meeting "the first evil," or "primusque malorum" (4.169), an event that changed the course of history by spelling the end of the Cartheginian empire and by making its conflict with Rome inevitable. For Dido, this event is equally fraught and ambiguous, with Virgil writing that she called the event "marriage" in order to hide her shame ["coniugium vocat, hoc praetexit nomine culpam" (4.172)]. See P. Vergili Maronis. *Aeneidos: Liber Quartus*, ed. R. G. Austin (Oxford: Oxford University Press, 1955).

24. Concepts of "race" and nation are difficult for this period. Most scholars agree that the term *gens*, while meaning family or a group related through blood or marriage, can also mean a "people" or was conceived of as a "race." Others agree that group identity at this time was linguistic and cultural identity. People saw themselves as belonging to the same group with people who spoke their own language, hence the Greek term "barbarian" for outsiders who simply did not speak Greek.

25. Robert Hanning's comments on the function of the Brut story represent well the traditional view of this kind of tale and its place in the overall narrative. Hanning writes that "Brut proceeds to an island home, far from the old world and there establishes a new, fertile nation." The Britons then become a "new order, free from the traditions of war and vengeance" and the *Historia regum Britanniae* becomes "an exultation of Britain" (*Vision of History*, 105). The story of Brutus's wandering and establishment of Britain re-affirms the Roman patriarchal social ideal and the illusion of continuity that was destroyed when Brutus killed his parents, a Roman history that was itself re-establishing the heritage of a fallen Troy.

26. Louise O. Fradenburg, with Carla Freccero, "The Pleasures of History," *Gay and Lesbian Quarterly* 1 (1995): 372.

27. See especially the death of Turnus in France. Griscom, ed., *Historia regum Britanniae*, 1.15; Thorpe, trans., *History of the Kings*, 71.

28. Fradenburg, with Freccero, "Pleasures of History," 372.

29. Parallel visions can be found in *Aeneid* 6 when the generations of Rome up to Augustus are revealed to Aeneas and in the third book of the *Faerie Queene*, when Britomart sees the lineage she creates with Artegall stretching forward to Queen Elizabeth.

30. Richard Waswo argues that this notion of civilization as something that must be transported from elsewhere is peculiarly Western. As he writes, "the Occident...had a choice of cultural ancestors....To fix on Troy, however, was to impose an origin that was always already destroyed, and hence required a narrative of displacement, exile, and reconstruction....The story is therefore structured as a journey, the search for a predestined and permanent home. The story thus presents civilization as that which comes from somewhere else." He argues that this pattern is one of the roots of imperialism and colonial attitudes, and has actually worked to create these concepts and events. While provocative, Waswo's interpretation of this narrative through Vergil, Geoffrey of Monmouth, and Spenser does not address how gender functions in this dynamic, a striking omission when one considers the structural centrality of such female figures as Creusa, Dido, and Lavinia in the Vergilian tradition. Waswo, "The History that Literature Makes," 546.

31. An interesting exception is the case of Assaracus, a bastard son of a Greek noble and his Trojan concubine. Although his deceased father has provided castles for Assaracus, the legitimate heir refuses to grant his half-brother's claim. In this instance, Assaracus invokes his mother's lineage, forming an

alliance with Brut not only to unseat Pandrasus, but to regain his own patrimony.

32. Hanning also describes the *Historia regum Britanniae*'s version of the legend of St. Ursula as pathetic. During Conon's colonization of Brittany, seventy-one thousand women, of all classes of England, are sent on a ship to become wives of the colonists. Geoffrey relates that they do not wish to go, due alternately to love of country or love of virginity. Ultimately, they face shipwreck on the German coast, as well as death or enslavement by the Huns who find them there. For his views on Ignoge and on Ursula, see *Vision of History*, 162; for Geoffrey's account of Ursula, see Griscom, ed., *Historia regum Britanniae*, 351; Thorpe, trans., *History of the Kings*, 142.

33. Rubin, "Traffic in Women," 182.

34. Lauretis, "Desire in Narrative," 132.

35. Griscom, ed., *Historia regum Britanniae*, 4.16.

36. Griscom, ed., *Historia regum Britanniae*, 2.4; Thorpe, trans., *History of the Kings*, 76–77.

37. Peggy McCracken examines how infanticide by mothers is always motivated by revenge in "Engendering Sacrifice: Blood, Lineage, and Infanticide in Old French Literature," *Speculum* 77 (2002): 55–75. For more generalized overviews of the ways mothers function in the middle ages see John Carmi Parsons and Bonnie Wheeler, eds., *Medieval Mothering* (New York: Garland, 1996) and John Carmi Parsons, ed., *Medieval Queenship* (New York: St. Martin's Press, 1993).

Chapter Two: Women's Patronage and the Writing of History: Nicholas Trevet's *Les Cronicles* and Geoffrey Chaucer's *Man of Law's Tale*

1. On the status of *Les Chronicles* as the first universal history in Anglo-Norman, see M. Dominica Legge, *Anglo-Norman Literature and Its Background* (Oxford: Clarendon Press, 1963), 301. Some scholars characterize universal history as being "providential history," that is, concerned with illustrating how the events of human history reveal God's plan for the world. This philosophy was ultimately gleaned from Augustine's notion of the two cities, the earthly and the heavenly, which mingle in the Christian world; see Taylor, *English Historical Literature*, 91. William J. Brandt, however, points out that "a universalizing chronicle is simply one which did not self-consciously pursue a single line of action, but moved along freely among a variety of interests"; see *The Shape of Medieval History: Studies in Modes of Perception* (New Haven: Yale University Press, 1966), 45.

2. See Joan Ferrante, *To the Glory of her Sex: Women's Roles in the Composition of Medieval Texts* (Bloomington: Indiana University Press, 1997), 39–40, for this concept.

3. See Robert Pratt, "Chaucer and *Les Cronicles* of Nicholas Trevet," in *Studies in Language, Literature and Culture of the Middle Ages and Later*, ed. E. Bagby Atwood and Archibald A. Hill (Austin: University of Texas Press, 1969), 303–11.

4. See Patterson, "Romance of History," 197–204 and Gabrielle Speigel, *Romancing the Past: The Rise of Vernacular Prose Historiography in Thirteenth-Century France* (Berkeley: University of California Press, 1993), 1–6.

5. Nicholas Trevet's (born c.1258–68) career and reputation were well-established long before his writing of *Les Cronicles* and his affiliation with Princess Mary. An English Dominican friar, his education, writings, and political connections placed him at the center of the literary and cultural world of the late thirteenth and early fourteenth centuries. His early education was in London, and he progressed through Oxford until he became a Master there. He studied in Paris and traveled to Italy. It is commonly believed that he became the Prior of Dominican house at Ludgate later in his life. Although Trevet's role in the Dominican order was that of a teacher, he was also a prolific and well-regarded scholar. His corpus of writings shows him to have been a "true polymath, being theologian, Biblicist, hebraist, historian, and classicist." See Beryl Smalley, quoted in Ruth J. Dean, "Nicholas Trevet, Historian," in *Medieval Learning and Literature: Essays Presented to Richard William Hunt*, ed. J. J. G. Alexander and M. T. Gibson (Oxford: Clarendon Press, 1976), 328; this account of Trevet's career relies heavily on Dean's work in this article. His religious works include Biblical commentaries on Leviticus, Wisdom, and the Psalms, as well as commentaries on later religious texts such as Augustine's *City of God*, and Boethius' *Consolation of Philosophy*. His classical scholarship encompassed commentaries on ancient writers such as Seneca, Ovid, and Livy.

In addition to these commentaries on early Christian and classical authors, Trevet wrote two Latin prose histories that predate the Anglo-Norman *Les Cronicles* (c. 1328–35). The first, the *Annales Sex Regum Angliae*, is an account of the British kings from Stephen to Edward I, written in about 1320 through 1323. Trevet's second Latin history, the *Historia ab orde condito ad Christi navitatem*, written about 1327–29, has a much broader scope than the *Annales*, relating the history of the world from its creation to the birth of Christ, spanning events from Biblical through Roman history, to early British legend. Trevet's source base in the *Historia* shows him to have been conversant with the mainstream historiography of his day. He includes important predecessors such as Peter Comestor's *Historia scholastica*, Augustine's *City of God*, Bede's *Historia Ecclesiastica*, Geoffrey of Monmouth's *Historia regum Britanniae*, and Livy's *Ab urbe condita*. Contemporary historians praised not only Trevet's accuracy in these two Latin chronicles, but also his lively and witty style. As an educated friar and scholar teaching at Oxford, Trevet occupied a prestigious place in his culture.

Trevet's importance, however, also extended to the Plantagenet court. His family connections may have given him access to aristocratic society in his earlier years, for his father, Thomas Trevet was a justice under both Henry III and Edward I. His histories themselves give the best evidence for his access to court culture for they were written at the request of patrons. Both the *Historia* and *Les Cronicles* include formal dedications and the *Annales* may have had royal patronage as well.

6. Fradenburg, with Carla Freccero, "Pleasures of History," 371; Walter J. Ong, "Latin Language Study as a Renaissance Puberty Rite," *Studies in Philology* 56 (1956): 103–24.

7. June Hall McCash, ed., *The Cultural Patronage of Medieval Women* (Athens: University of Georgia Press, 1996), 14.

8. Miriam Shadis, "Piety, Politics, and Power: The Patronage of Leonor of England and Her Daughters Berenguela of Leon and Blanche of Castile," in *The Cultural Patronage of Medieval Women*, ed. June Hall McCash (Athens: University of Georgia Press, 1996), 203.

9. Speigel, *Romancing the Past*, 77, 92–93.

10. John Carmi Parsons, "Of Queens, Courts, and Books: Reflections on the Literary Patronage of Thirteenth-Century Plantagenet Queens," in *The Cultural Patronage of Medieval Women*, ed. June Hall McCash (Athens: University of Georgia Press, 1996), 181.

11. McCash, *Cultural Patronage*, 14, 22–23; Susan Groag Bell, "Medieval Women Book Owners: Arbiters of Lay Piety and Ambassadors of Culture," *Signs* 7 (1982): 163.

12. Parsons, "Of Queens, Courts, and Books," 185.

13. Ibid., 199 n. 156.

14. Ibid., 178 n. 17, 179.

15. Bell, "Medieval Women Book Owners," 155.

16. Karen K. Jambeck, "Patterns of Women's Literary Patronage: England, 1200–ca. 1475," in *The Cultural Patronage of Medieval Women*, ed. June Hall McCash (Athens: University of Georgia Press, 1996), 236, 242.

17. Parsons, "Of Queens, Courts, and Books," 178.

18. Ibid., 186.

19. Lines in Old French from *Les Chronicles* are taken from Alexander Rutherford, "The Anglo-Norman Chronicle of Nicholas Trevet: Text with Historical, Philological, and Literary Study" (Diss. University of London, 1932). Those in Middle English are taken from Christine M. Rose, "An edition of Houghton Library FMS 938: The Fifteenth-Century Middle English Translation of Nicholas Trevet's "Les Cronicles," with "Brut" Continuation" (Diss. Tufts University, 1985). See Dean, "Nicholas Trevet," 340, 347, as well as her "The Manuscripts of Nicholas Trevet's Anglo-Norman Chronicles," *Medievalia et Humanistica* 14 (1962): 95–105, for her evaluations of the dedication and the manuscripts.

20. There is some disagreement among scholars regarding dedications and what they may signify about patronage practice. Some accept dedications as proof of patronage, but Diana B. Tyson urges that more evidence be required such as "mention by author of payment, record of payment, praise of the patron, introduction or epilogue addressed to him, internal evidence such as structure or treatment of subject matter, existence of a presentation copy, illumination, and most important of all, a statement by the author that he was asked to write the work." See Diana B. Tyson, "Patronage of French Vernacular History Writers in the Twelfth and Thirteenth Centuries," *Romania* 100

(1979): 184–5. McCash comments that Tyson's high standards of evidence are certainly desirable, but that realistically, a dedication is often the only clue scholars have to patronage, and that it is "probably stronger for women than for men, for writers would have little else to gain from most female dedicatees than their patronage." McCash also points out that given the time consuming nature of literary production in the middle ages, dedications "would scarcely have been made lightly." See McCash, *Cultural Patronage*, 2–3 for both points. It is important, however, to read a dedication to a female patron as a complex social act for as Roberta Krueger points out in her study of Old French romance, the presence of dedications to women does not prove for romance at least, that "individual female patrons exerted a formative influence .. . or that the genre promoted women's interests." In fact, "women's privileged status in the frame of the romance accompanied her *displacement* from legal and social society." See Krueger, *Women Readers*, 2–3.

21. Parsons, "Of Queens, Courts, and Books," 199 n. 55.

22. Dean, "Nicholas Trevet," 340.

23. Ibid., 336.

24. Perhaps one reason this history was well-received was the way Trevet tailored it to his specifically aristocratic audience. Trevet explains his concern for this courtly reading audience in short prefatory remarks to his history. He is a sympathetic author—since he has heard that readers can become annoyed at the great length of historical works ["Purce qe nous sumes avisez de ceux qe sont perceous en estudies q'il sont enoiez de la prolixete d'estories" (Rutherford, "Anglo-Norman Chronicle," 2.1)], he will attempt to set down events of the past briefly, but without "shortening the truth" ["ne nous n'escourterom pas la verite de l'estoire" (Rutherford, "Anglo-Norman Chronicle," 2.1)]. He anticipates his audiences' lack of books and learning and seeks to write a text that will fill this gap ["et qe plusurs en ount defaute des livres, il nous plust requiller brevement la conte des lynes qe descenderent del primer piere Adam" (Rutherford, "Anglo-Norman Chronicle," 2.1)]. Scholars have interpreted these remarks in various ways, ranging from Rutherford and Legge who maintain that Trevet wrote his text to entertain, as a kind of epitome or popularization of world history to more recent scholars such as Rose who detect a kind of moral didacticism more reflective of traditional universal histories, especially when Trevet hopes that an appeal to the heart will enable the mind to hold his meaning more quickly and easily ["si qe par la descripcion q'est mise soient les coers plus attraitz a regarder a l'abreggement faite, qe l'em puisse la chose de plus legier entendre et retenir de plus vive memoire" (Rutherford, "Anglo-Norman Chronicle," 2.1)]. See Legge, *Anglo-Norman Literature*, 301.

Trevet's concern for his rather secular, aristocratic audience markedly influenced his method of composition, his use of sources, and his style of writing. *Les Cronicles* is far less technical than Trevet's earlier work; the text leaves out most citations and many dates, opting instead for formulaic and patrinomial phrases; see Dean, "Nicholas Trevet," 342. Although Rutherford calls Trevet's method of compilation a "mosaic," noting that there are often many sources in the same paragraph, giving the history a "patchwork appearance" (1.55). As exhaustive as Trevet's sourcebase was, he consistently worked the material for his audience's benefit, translating Latin quotations and explaining names (1.47), adding such "picturesque" detail as the very time of day at which Adam and Eve leave paradise (1.38), and lastly, digressing time and again into anecdotes (1.40). Although Rose finds little dialogue or drama in these details and anecdotes (xlv) and thinks that the repetition of introductory phrases such as "after that," or "in the year after that," creates a "piling up of events and names...and often the text of the chronicle is really a list or genealogy" (xlvi), she notes that Trevet's organizational schema of books, "chapitres," and cross-references, does give a "sense of plan and revision." As Rose explains, the "effect of recapitulation and previewing of material is to lend a more polished and seamless tone to the work than we might expect from its often jumbled and choppy entries" (xlv). See Rose, "Edition of the Houghton Library FMS 938."

Ruth Dean finds persuasive evidence for Trevet developing a distinct compositional style in light of the new audience for his vernacular history, arguing that

> it is evident from the outset that he is writing now for a person or persons whose background and interests are quite different from those of the readers for whom he composed the *Historia*. Here are no metaphysical calculations, following Bede, as to whether earthly Time began with the *Fiat Lux* or with the creation of sun and moon and stars on the fourth day, such as open the *Historia*. This is a straightforward account from Genesis (see her "Nicholas Trevet," 341).

This method, along with the emphasis on anecdote and detail described by Rutherford, prove for Dean that Trevet is endeavoring to write a different kind of text for his new, more secular audience, one that included women readers and one that needed vernacular texts to gain the historical knowledge in such political vogue at court.

25. Dean, "Nicholas Trevet," 348–49.
26. Dean, "Nicholas Trevet," 340, 347 and her "Manuscripts of Nicholas Trevet," 95–105.
27. For the quote above see Pratt, "Chaucer and *Les Chronicles*," 311. On Chaucer's historical knowledge see Pratt, "Chaucer and *Les Chronicles*," 303, 309 and Robert M. Correale, "Chaucer's Manuscript of Nicholas Trevet's *Les Cronicles*," *Chaucer Review* 25.3 (1991): 238–65.
28. Mary of Woodstock's house at Amesbury could have exerted such feminine influence over how history was shaped and written; as Pamela Sheingorn suggests, in addition to Mary's patronage of Trevet's history, there is evidence that the *Imola Psalter*, a thirteenth-century text that highlights St. Anne, was also produced for a nun of Amesbury. For the quoted text, as well as information on Amesbury and the *Imola Psalter*, see Pamela Sheingorn, "The Holy Kinship: The Ascendency of Matriliny in Sacred Genealogy of the Fifteenth Century," *Thought* 64.254 (September 1989): 271. Also see Sheingorn, "Appropriating the Holy Kinship: Gender and Family History," in *In-*

terpreting Cultural Symbols: Saint Anne in Late Medieval Society*, ed. Kathleen Ashley and Pamela Sheingorn (Athens: University of Georgia Press, 1990), 169–98.

29. Ferrante, *To The Glory*, 8.

30. Ferrante further explains that these readers would have taken "pride in the accomplishments of other women, in the present as well as in the past: queens look to the achievements of their mothers and grandmothers, abbesses to their illustrious fellows." She concludes that these histories accept women with positions of authority in the past, just as their patrons possess in the present, and that these female figures are "seen as a normal, even essential part of history." See Ferrante, *To the Glory*, 8, 106.

31. See Rutherford, "Anglo-Norman Chronicle," 1.13–16, for a more detailed description of the chronicle.

32. An error on Trevet's part. Lot's incest with his daughters is not omitted, but told in Genesis 19: 30–38.

33. For both quotes, see Sheingorn, "Holy Kinship," 171. Sheingorn goes further with this argument, stating that the prominence of St. Anne may point to an alternate matrilineal trinity that emphasized Christ's physical body as opposed to the divine soul. This incarnational theology would privilege a maternal family on earth, glorifying motherhood and making it a female role to be respected even by the convent-bound. Sheingorn cites David Herlihy, *Medieval Households*, 122–24, as illustrating the growing status of motherhood in the late middle ages, both with demographic evidence as well as in the portraits in didactic literature and saints' lives.

34. Freidrich W. D. Brie, ed. *Brut, or the Chronicles of England*, Early English Text Society, os 131, 136. (London: Kegan Paul, 1906–1908) will be the focus of Chapter Three of this study.

35. My thanks to Christine Rose for sharing her knowledge of these manuscripts with me. See also Dean, "Nicholas Trevet," 345, as well as her "Manuscripts of Nicholas Trevet," 104, regarding these genealogies.

36. Herlihy, *Medieval Households*, 82, 83. The agnatic kinship can be further distinguished from the cognatic as a system regulating inheritance, rather than blood relation. Herlihy and most historians also see the culture surrounding this family narrative as very much focussed on origins and family pride. For a detailed discussion of these lineage types and their relation to social change and marrige practice, see *Medieval Households*, 79–111. For Georges Duby's conclusion that the patrilineal agnatic lineage supplanted the cognatic form, see Duby, *The Knight, the Lady*.

37. See Rutherford, "Anglo-Norman Chronicle," 2.337–352; Rose, "Edition of Houghton Library FMS 938," 365–74. Ferrante finds this focus on family typical of histories written under the auspices of female patronage, pointing out that these texts "focus on human relations to see the family more as the center of historic events." See Ferrante, *To the Glory*, 69.

38. Rutherford, "Anglo-Norman Chronicle," 2.346–47; Rose, "Edition of Houghton Library FMS 938," 368.

39. Trevet plays on Mary's name a bit here, praising her connection to two Biblical Marys: the mother of God who wed the king of Heaven, and Mary, the sister of Martha, who chose the contemplative life of listening to the words of Jesus, unlike Martha who cooked and prepared meals for the apostles.

40. This scholarship branches widely. Traditional strains examine the *Man of Law's Tale* as either an ironic tale whose telling reveals the pomposity of its teller—Walter Scheps, "Chaucer's *Man of Law* and the Tale of Constance," *PMLA* 89 (1974): 285–95; Alfred David, "The Man of Law vs. Chaucer: A Case in Poetics," *PMLA* 82 (1967): 217–25; Rodney Delasanta, "And of Great Reverence: Chaucer's Man of Law," *Chaucer Review* 5.4 (1971): 288–310; Morton Bloomfield, "The *Man of Law's Tale*: A Tragedy of Victimization and a Christian Comedy," *PMLA* 87 (1972): 384–90 —or as a didactic narrative— Kevin Roddy, "Mythic Sequence in the *Man of Law's Tale*," *Journal of Medieval and Renaissance Studies* 10.1 (1980): 1–22; V. A. Kolve, *Chaucer and the Imagery of Narrative* (Stanford: Stanford University Press, 1984). More recent emphases include commerce, Laurel L. Hendrix, "'Pennannce profytable': The Currency of Custance in Chaucer's *Man of Law's Tale*," *Exemplaria* 6.1 (Spring 1994): 141–66; Christopher Bracken, "Constance and the Silkweavers: Working Women and Colonial Fantasy in Chaucer's *Man of Law's Tale*," *Princeton Journal of Women, Gender, and Culture* 8.1 (1994): 13–39; R. A. Shoaf, "'Unwemmed Custance': Circulation, Property, and Incest in the *Man of Law's Tale*," *Exemplaria* 2.1 (March 1990): 287–302, orientalism, Susan Schibanoff, "Worlds Apart: Orientalism, Antifeminism, and Heresy in Chaucer's *Man of Law's Tale*," *Exemplaria* 8.1 (Spring 1996): 59–96, and storytelling David Weisberg, "Telling Stories About Constance: Framing and Narrative Strategy in the *Canterbury Tales*," *Chaucer Review* 27.1 (1992): 45–64. Feminist interpretations examine Constance as one among Chaucer's many female figures: Julliette Dor, "From the Crusading Virago to the Polysemous Virgin: Chaucer's Constance," in *A Wife There Was* (Liege, Belgium: Universite de Liege, 1992), 129–40; J. Stephen Russell, "Dido, Emily, and Constance: Femininity and Subversion in the Mature Chaucer," *Medieval Perspectives* 1.1 (Spring 1986), ed. Pedro F. Campa, Charles W. Conwell, Robert J. Vallier: 65–73; Sheila Delany, "Womanliness in the *Man of Law's Tale*" *Chaucer Review* 9.1 (1974): 63–71. Source study provides a foundation for many of these approaches as some scholars trace folkloric antecedents for buried incest themes, wicked mothers-in-law, and monster children: Margaret Schlauch, *Chaucer's Constance and Accursed Queens* (New York: New York University Press, 1927; reprint New York: Gordian Press, 1969); Margaret Schlauch, "The Man of Law's Tale," in *Sources and Analogues of Chaucer's "Canterbury Tales"* ed. W. F. Bryan and G. Dempster (Chicago: University of Chicago Press, 1941), 155–206; Elizabeth Archibald, "The Flight from Incest: Two Classical Precursors of the Constance Theme," *Chaucer Review* 20.4 (1986): 259–72; Thomas Hanks, "*Emare*: An Influence on the *Man of Law's Tale*," *Chaucer Review* 18.2 (1983): 182–86; Wintrop Wetherbee, "Constance and the World in Chaucer and Gower," in *John Gower: Recent Readings*, ed. R. F. Yeager (Kalamazoo, MI: Western Michigan University, 1989), 65–93. Clark and Wasserman argue that Chaucer's changes to this tale highlight Constance as a woman undergo-

ing a matriarchal rite of passage, emphasizing her trials, but that the tale paradoxically illustrates the rise of patriarchy in the birth of an heir like Maurice. See their "Constance as Romance and Folk Heroine in Chaucer's *Man of Law's Tale*," *Rice University Studies* 64 (1978): 13–24. Others have examined the triad of Trevet-Gower-Chaucer, reaching a consensus that while Chaucer knew Gower's tale of Constance in the *Confessio Amantis*, his primary source for the *Man of Law's Tale* was Nicholas Trevet's Anglo-Norman history, *Les Cronicles*. See Robert M. Correale, "Gower's Source Manuscript of Nicholas Trevet's *Les Cronicles*," in *John Gower: Recent Readings*, ed. R. F. Yeager (Kalamazoo, MI: Western Michigan University, 1989), 133–57; Peter Nicholson, "Chaucer Borrows from Gower: The Sources of the *Man of Law's Tale*," in *Chaucer and Gower: Difference, Mutuality, and Exchange English Literature Series* (Victoria, BC: University of Victoria, 1991), 85–99; Peter Nicholson, "The *Man of Law's Tale*: What Chaucer Really Owed to Gower," *Chaucer Review* 26.2 (1991): 153–74.

41. For an opposing view see Nicholson, "Chaucer Borrows from Gower," 86–90, especially. n. 15, who argues that Gower's version is more important to Chaucer than Trevet's and so downplays the centrality of the Tale of Constance. He argues against Pratt, that *Les Cronicles* could not have been widely known to the royal family or to Chaucer. Also see Phillip Wynn, "The Conversion Story in Nicholas Trevet's "Tale of Constance," *Viator* 13 (1984): 259–74, who defends "history" as a discourse and practice, arguing that the emphases of literary critics are misplaced and that Trevet must have included the tale of Constance in his history simply because he found it in a now-lost source and considered it to be historical.

42. See Rose, "Edition of Houghton Library FMS 938," lxx–lxxl.

43. Kolve is nearly unique in noting that among the genres for the *Man of Law's Tale* discussed by its critics, folktale, romance, marvelous tale, or saint's life, medieval audiences would have seen this tale as history. To him, this recognition represents a fourteenth-century cultural practice of turning to the past to glean a moral lesson, in this case from when Britain was first converted to Christianity. See Kolve, *Chaucer and the Imagery of Narrative*, 297–99.

44. Even though Mary of Woodstock was an unmarried nun who was never compelled to leave her birth family's court to marry a foreign king, her immediate family was filled both with women who entered the British court from afar and with sisters who left home to wed abroad; see Parsons, "Of Queens, Courts, and Books," 175–201. The tale of Constance as written by Trevet under Mary's patronage becomes almost a fantasy for these so-called "diplomatic brides."

45. Constance as introduced by Trevet is a very different figure than Chaucer's Custance. Because she is her father's only child, she is educated in Christian faith, the seven sciences, and "en diverses langages" (2.201.12). When she first meets the Syrian merchants, she preaches [ele...lour precha (2.201.17)] Christianity to them until they convert. Chaucer reduces this account, with the merchants hearing and seeing only her beauty, youth, humility, courtesy, and holiness, and passing this report on to the Syrian sultan, without them-

selves being converted. Such reduction on Chaucer's part, as told by the Man of Law, continues upon her arrival in Northumberland. Kolve observes that for the *Man of Law's Tale* the image that most immediately comes to mind is that of a woman in a rudderless boat; Kolve, *Chaucer and the Imagery of Narrative*, 302. No such image dominates Trevet's version, partly because of his paratactic style which accords each event equal emphasis. The image of the rudderless boat is not repeated often nor is it described elaborately enough to make it the dominant image in the story or even the dominant conception of the heroine, Constance. Trevet describes how the Sultaness and her mariners leave her "a quatre venz" but states simply that "Dieux estoit soun mariner" (2.204.27–28). God was her companion, giving her comfort and counsel, until finally he sends a favorable wind to take the ship to Northumbria. Constance is implicitly compared to the patriarch Noah, as Trevet writes "Dieux, qi governa le nef le seint homme Noe en le grant deluvie, maunda un vent covenable... ariva la nef la veille de la Nativite Nostre Seignur Jesu Crist" (2.205.1–5) ["god the whyche gouerned that holy mannys shyp Noe in the grete diluuie that ys to say Noes flood sent a wynde full propise and couenable...And the shyp arryved and come to londe on Crystemas euen" (218.9–12)]. This account is matter-of-fact, providing a transition from one part of the story to another, much unlike the Man of Law's excessive rhetorical performance so familiar to Chaucerian scholars which serves to create the image of the abject and passive women who spends years in the rudderless boat. French quotes above have been taken from Rutherford, "Anglo-Norman Chronicle"; those in Middle English from Rose, "Edition of Houghton Library FMS 938." On the Man of Law's apostrophe on Custance set adrift in the rudderless boat see William C. Johnson, Jr., "*The Man of Law's Tale*: Aesthetics and Christianity in Chaucer," *Chaucer Review* 16.3 (1982): 201–221, who argues that in this, as in each of Chaucer's additions to Trevet, Chaucer amplifies Constance's victimization. On Chaucer's characterization of Constance, Wetherbee comments that Chaucer's "heroine bathes in 'pitee' at every opportunity"; Wetherbee, "Constance and the World," 75. Russell reads Constance as a figure of resignation in these added speeches; Russell, "Dido, Emily, and Constance," 65–73.

46. Feminist criticism of Chaucer's tale, however, has thus far been unconscious of the potential ramifications of Chaucer's diminution of Trevet's central heroine. Carolyn Dinshaw seeks to recoup a bit of selfhood for the blank figure of Constance, arguing that not only does she hold an awareness of herself in the community of Christian women, Constance also has a "definite ability to shape her life as a perfect romance to write in a sense her own history." Dinshaw accedes, however, that even the furtive attempts at self-definition that she charts in Chaucer's tale "serve patriarchy well," for Constance's consciousness is allotted to her by the Man of Law speaking her and allows her only to experience suffering and constraint. See Carolyn Dinshaw, "The Man of Law and Its 'Abhomynacions'" in *Chaucer's Sexual Poetics* (Madison, WI: University of Wisconsin, 1989). Dinshaw fails to note that these moments of self-definition are some of the most important traces of Trevet's heroine, of a figure whose statements and actions take place as part of a col-

lection that narrates women as important ingredients of history, not as epitomes of human suffering and passivity.

One critic who focuses more explicitly on the role of storytelling in the *Man of Law's Tale,* David Weisberg, argues along with Marshall H. Leicester Jr., *The Disenchanted Self: Representing the Subject in the "Canterbury Tales"* (Berkeley: University of California Press, 1990) that throughout the *Canterbury Tales* the character of tellers is spelled out by their acts of telling—that the *Canterbury Tales* is a discourse that creates the narrating subject. In particular, the Man of Law creates a "tale of conflicting tellers"; everyone from the Syrian merchants, to the Northumbrian knight, Alla's constable and his mother Donegild, tells a particular version of Constance. These narratives become "foisted against a body that must live the events that fulfill that narrative"; Weisberg, "Telling Stories about Constance," 57. In the *Man of Law's Tale,* the figure of Constance then becomes one of suffering, humility, and endurance. This process does not occur in Chaucer's source.

47. As Richard Waswo has recently argued, this kind of link allows Britain to be the peer of Rome, figuring them together as equals in historical and narrative world power. See his "Our Ancestors," 272.

48. Schlauch explores this tension by using Frazierian anthropology to probe the history of the "calumnated queen," usually a young, newly married woman and her offspring who are ostracized by the mother-in-law, but Schlauch also charts incestuous behavior by kings toward their daughters. Schlauch attributes these themes to a now questioned theory of an early European shift from matriarchy to patriarchy in which the real political power of the king's mother is displaced. As Schlauch puts it, "we have stepmothers and mothers-in-law and witches and fathers who are cruel because their fear is great"; see her *Chaucer's Constance,* 61. Also see her article, "The Man of Law's Tale." Wynn argues against Schlauch that Trevet's tale is one of conversion and that possible analogues exist in Arabic texts. Wynn vigorously defends Trevet from any charges of fiction-making in his history. Wynn, "Conversion Story," 259–74.

49. Quotations from the *Man of Law's Tale* from taken from Larry D. Benson, ed., *The Riverside Chaucer,* 3rd ed. (Boston: Houghton Mifflin Co., 1987). Raybin argues that this concealment of her identity in the *Man of Law's Tale* makes her "in a world of masculine values, the consummate outsider" for this concealment allows her to be idealized as constancy and spirituality; David Raybin, "Custance and History: Woman as Outsider in Chaucer's *Man of Law's Tale," Studies in the Age of Chaucer* 12 (1990): 70. Schibanoff also uses this crux to illustrate the "foreign" status of Constance, a status that she argues combines with the Orientalism of the tale to create an othered discourse that bonds the Canterbury pilgrims together in a fellowship of men. Schibanoff, "World's Apart," 59–96. In Trevet, however, concealment actually allows Constance's true noble status to be recognized and she does become an integrated part of the royal family and Northumbrian society.

50. The other important instance of Constance's active intervention is, of course, when she pushes the prospective rapist overboard during her travels from Northumbria back to Rome. Protecting herself from assault not only protects her own identity as a holy woman, it also preserves her as an unchallenged conduit of Alle's lineage and her father's.

51. Dinshaw, "Man of Law and Its 'Abhomynacions,'" 109.

52. Cf. Chaucer's version here. Dawson argues that her "rhetoric of victimization actually reverses the power roles" between Custance and her father; Robert B. Dawson, "Constance in Context: Rethinking the Protagonist of the *Man of Law's Tale*," *Chaucer Review* 26.3 (1992): 299–300.

Chapter Three: Reading the Past in 1400: *Sir Gawain and the Green Knight* and the Middle English Prose *Brut* Chronicle

1. Tolkien's note on line 2523 of his edition, "the Brutus bokez therof beres wyttenesse," argues that the phrase "Brutus bokez" "might be applied to any chronicles or romances of British times, not necessarily devoted to the legendary history of Brutus" and that for the Welsh, the term *brud* became a way to denote a chronicle generally. Scholars have, I think, too easily accepted this disclaimer, and have neglected situating the poem in the context of contemporary Brut histories. See J. R. R. Tolkien and E. V. Gordon, eds., *Sir Gawain and the Green Knight* 2nd ed., rev., Norman Davis (Oxford: Clarendon Press, 1967), 131.

2. In spite of the documented popularity of the *Brut* in the fourteenth and fifteenth centuries, medievalists have failed nearly universally to examine this narrative for anything other than linguistic studies. Lister M. Matheson and John Taylor each argue that the *Brut*, along with Froissart's *Chroniques* and Ranulf Higden's *Polychronicon*, not only dominate the field of medieval chronicles, but that their appeal to readers lay at least partly in their literary content. See Taylor, *English Historical Literature*, 56–58; Matheson, "King Arthur," 253. See also Denys Hay, *Annalists and Historians: Western Historiography from the Eighth to the Eighteenth Centuries* (London: Methuen, 1977) and Ernst Breisach, *Historiography: Ancient, Medieval, and Modern* (Chicago: University of Chicago Press, 1983). Matheson further observes that the "paucity of studies dealing with the *Brut* has prevented many modern scholars from fully realizing its central position"; see Lister M. Matheson, "Historical Prose," in *Middle English Prose*, ed. A. S. G. Edwards (New Brunswick: Rutgers University Press, 1984), 214.

   Much of the argument for the *Brut's* popularity rests upon the large number of extant manuscripts, as well as the number that are mentioned in wills and other documents. Matheson lists 160 manuscripts of the Middle English translation of the prose *Brut*, with fifty more of the Anglo-Norman version and fifteen in Latin. See Matheson, "Historical Prose," 210. For a comprehensive list of manuscripts see Lister M. Matheson, "The Middle English Prose *Brut*: A Location List of the Manuscripts and Early Printed Editions," *Analytical & Enumerative Bibliography* 3 (1979): 254–66. John Taylor, "The French 'Brut' and the Reign of Edward II, "*English Historical Review* 77 (1987): 423–37, agrees that Matheson's list supercedes that of Friedrich W. D. Brie, *Geschichte und Quellen der mittelenglischen Prosa-chronick "The Brute of England" oder "The Chronicles of England"* (Marburg: N. G. Elwert'sche Verlagsbuchhandlung, 1905). For information on wills see Antonia Gransden, *Historical Writing in England, c. 1307–1600* (Ithaca: Cornell University Press, 1986). Edward Donald Kennedy also provides a cogent description of the text's history in his edition of *Chronicles and Other Historical Writing*, vol. 8. *Manual of the Writings in Middle English, 1050–1500*, ed. Albert E. Hartung (Hamden, CT: Archon Books, 1989).

Critics and historians alike agree upon the influence of the prose *Brut*. With the advent of printing, the *Brut*, under the name *Chronicles of England*, became the first chronicle to be produced by Caxton, going through thirteen editions from 1480 to 1528; see Matheson, "Historical Prose," 210. Through these editions "the *Brut* reached the Tudors, to be plundered by the historians Edward Hall and Raphael Holinshed and through them to provide Shakespeare with copy"; Gransden, *English Historical Writing in England, c. 1307–1600*, 223. In the fourteenth century, the text was first circulated in French, but after 1333, this text was superceded by its English translation; see Taylor, "French 'Brut,'" 119. According to Brie, the English translation was compiled between 1350 and 1380; see his *Geschichte und Quellen*, 54. Robert A. Albano surveys the textual history of the *Brut* in Chapter Two of his *Middle English Historiography* (New York: Peter Lang, 1993).

Matheson is currently preparing a more modern and definitive text of *Brut*. Until his work is finished, however, the most readily available text of the prose *Brut* is F. W. D. Brie's EETS edition of 1906. This edition depends primarily upon MS Rawlinson B171, with the opening tales of Albine and of Brut's wanderings taken from MS Douce 323, the beginning of Rawlinson B171 being heavily damaged. Matheson critiques Brie's classification of the *Brut* corpus on a number of grounds. First, Brie examined only 147 of the 167 manuscripts personally and the reports he received about other manuscripts have been found to be erroneous. Second, Brie based his classification upon the number and type of continuations found in each manuscript. For Matheson, this is tantamount to classifying merely on similarity of content, instead of relying upon detailed textual and linguistic analysis. Until Matheson's project sees publication, however, scholars must use the EETS edition if they are to examine this important narrative. See Matheson, "Historical Prose," 211–12. Brie's classification appears in *Geschicte und Quellen*, 1 n. 1. An updated version was planned for volume three of the EETS edition, but was never completed.

The overall structure of Rawlinson B171 shows some interesting emphases. The first third is a fairly compressed version of early British history from the travels of Brut, through the conflicts with Rome, to the reign of Arthur. This section retells the bulk of Geoffrey Monmouth's *Historia regum Britanniae*. Following Mordred's defeat, the text turns to a brief survey of incidents from Anglo-Saxon history, mentioning the story of Havelock, Pope Gregory's observations on the angelic English, and the writing of English history by King Alfred. The rest of the manuscript, fully half the text, traces Plantagenet history from the conquest through the early reign of Edward III.

The last half of the text is also the most detailed narrative, recounting vast military campaigns against the Welsh and the Scots, as well as painting vivid portraits of such kings as Henry II, Edward I, and Edward III. The text ends with the English victorious over the Scots at the Battle of Halidon Hill in 1332.

3. Bergren, "Language and the Female," 74.

4. Louise Olga Fradenburg, ed., "Introduction: Rethinking Queenship," in *Women and Sovereignty* (Edinburgh: Edinburgh University Press, 1992), 7.

5. Speigel, "Genealogy," 45–53.

6. John Carmi Parsons, "Ritual and Symbol in the English Medieval Queenship to 1500," in *Women and Sovereignty*, ed. Louise Olga Fradenburg (Edinburgh: Edinburgh University Press, 1992), 9.

7. All citations from the prose *Brut* are taken from Brie's edition. Thorns and eths have been transcribed as "th."

8. The *Brut* elsewhere uses family imagery to express social peace and security, celebrating the kingship of Henry III, describing this role as a father to his kingdom by saying that "fram the tyme that Kyng Henry deide, til that Sire Edward was croned Kyng, all the gret Lordes oof Engeland were as faderles children, without eny socour that ham might mayntaene and gouerne, and defende aȝeynȝ her dedeliche enemys" (178).

9. "Cumque uxores non habentes, filias & cognatas britonum ab illis petiuissent, dedignati sunt britones huiusmodi populo natas suas maritare" (Griscom, *Historia regum Britanniae*, 327) ["Since they had no wives, the Picts asked the Britons for their daughters and kinswomen, but the Britons refused to marry off their womenfolk to such manner of men" (Thorpe, *History of the Kings*, 123)]; *Brut*: "But thai nade no wymmen amonges ham, and the Britons wolde nouȝt ȝeue here douȝtres to tho Straungers" (36).

10. According to Brie, two other MSS record this as: "amonges ham forto fiȝt that best mow" (50 varient 27).

11. For other treatments of this theme see: Sunhee Kim Gertz, "*Translatio studii et imperii*: Sir Gawain as Literary Critic," *Semiotica* 63 1/2 (1987): 185–203; Roy Liuzza, "Names, Reputation, and History in *Sir Gawain and the Green Knight*," *Essays in Medieval Studies: Proceedings of the Illinois Medieval Association* 6 (1989): 41–56; Malcolm Andrew, "The Fall of Troy in *Sir Gawain and the Green Knight* and *Troilus and Criseyde*," in *The European Tragedy of Troilus*, ed. Piero Boitani (Oxford: Clarendon, 1989), 75–93; Theodore Silverstein, "*Sir Gawain*, Dear Brutus, and Britain's Fortune Founding: A Study in Comedy and Convention," *Modern Philology* 62 (February 1963): 189–206.

12. Alfred David, "Gawain and Aeneas," *English Studies* 49.4 (August 1968): 407–08.

13. Sheila Fisher, "Leaving Morgan Aside: Women, History, and Revisionism in *Sir Gawain and the Green Knight*," in *The Passing of Arthur: New Essays in Arthurian Tradition*, ed. Christopher Baswell and William Sharpe (New York: Garland, 1988), 146.

14. Gayle Margherita, "Father Aeneas or Morgan the Goddess," in *The Romance of Origins: Language and Sexual Difference in Middle English Literature* (Philadelphia: University of Pennsylvania Press, 1994), 149.

15. Ibid., 143.

16. For a survey of criticism on this speech, see Julian Wasserman and Robert Blanch, "Gawain's Anti-Feminism: From Gollancz and Tolkein to the Millennium," *Medieval Perspectives* 15.2 (Fall 2000): 21–33.

17. Lines from *Gawain and the Green Knight* are taken from Tolkein's edition. Thorns and eths have been transliterated as "th."

18. McCracken, "Body Politic," 40.

19. On Arthur's presumed place in this tradition, see S. L. Clark and Julian N. Wasserman, "Gawain's Anti-Feminism Reconsidered," *JRMMRA* 6 (1985): 57–70.

20. Geraldine Heng argues that through the association of Mary and the knotted symbol of the Pentangle, the text tries to authorize a "particular fantasy of identity" by "allegorizing the linking up of all points of Gawain's imaginary subjectivity." This process of the pentangle's imagery "leads back inexorably, umbilically, via the route of an uncut knot, the pentangle to the (divine) mother whose image appears on the other side." See her "Feminine Knots and the Other in *Sir Gawain and the Green Knight*," *PMLA* 106.3 (May 1991): 500–14.

21. Fisher, for instance, argues that both Morgan and Guenevere partake in the Lady's actions in the center of the poem.

Conclusion

1. Jane Austen, *Persuasion* (New York: Alfred A. Knopf, Inc. 1906), 1.

2. Ibid., 7.

3. As Denise Riley argues, "'women' is historically, discursively constructed, and always relative to other categories which themselves change; 'women' is a volatile collectivity in which female persons can be very differently positioned, so that the apparent continuity of the subject of 'women'...can't provide an ontological foundation" (18). Diana Fuss argues cogently, however, that such "historicism," "constructivism," and "specificity" does not adequately diffuse charges of essentialism when taking women as objects of study. Rather, they simply disperse essentialism "through a number of micro-political units or sub-categorical classifications, each presupposing its own unique interior composition or metaphysical core" (20). Feminist scholars, in her eyes, should continually re-interrogate how essential categories impinge on their projects, rather than attempting to perform an analysis that excludes or believes it can work outside these categories. See Denise Riley, "Does A Sex Have a History?" in *Feminism and History*, ed. Joan Wallach Scott (Oxford: Oxford University Press, 1996), 18 and Diana Fuss, *Essentially Speaking: Feminism, Nature, and Difference* (New York: Routledge, 1989), 20.

BIBLIOGRAPHY

Primary Documents

Austen, Jane. *Persuasion.* New York: Alfred A. Knopf, 1906.

Benson, Larry D., ed. *The Riverside Chaucer,* 3rd ed. Boston: Houghton Mifflin Co., 1987.

Brie, Freidrich W. D., ed. *Brut, or the Chronicles of England.* Early English Text Society. OS 131, 136. London: Kegan Paul, 1906–1908.

Faral, Edmond, ed. *Historia regum Britanniae.* In *La Legende arthurienne— Etdues and documents.* 3 vols. Paris: Champion, 1929.

Griscom, Acton, ed. *The Historia Regum Britanniae of Geoffrey of Monmouth.* London: Longmans, Green and Co., 1929. Reprint Geneva: Slatkine Reprints, 1977.

Hammer, Jacob, ed. *The Historia Regum Britanniae of Geoffrey of Monmouth: A Varient Version.* Publications of the Medieval Academy of America. 57. Cambridge, MA: Medieval Academy of America, 1951.

Livy. *The Early History of Rome.* Translated by Aubrey de Selincourt. New York: Penguin Books, 1960.

Rose, Christine M. "An edition of Houghton Library FMS 938: The Fifteenth-Century Middle English Translation of Nicholas Trevet's "Les Cronicles," with "Brut" Continuation." Diss. Tufts University, 1985.

Rutherford, Alexander. "The Anglo-Norman Chronicle of Nicholas Trevet: Text with Historical, Philological, and Literary Study." Diss. University of London, 1932.

Thorpe, Lewis, trans. *History of the Kings of Britain by Geoffrey of Monmouth.* London: Penguin Books, 1966.

Tolkien, J. R. R. and E. V. Gordon, eds. *Sir Gawain and the Green Knight.* 2nd ed. Revised by Norman Davis. Oxford: Clarendon Press, 1967.

Vergili, P. Maronis. *Aeneidos: Liber Quartus.* Edited by R. G. Austin. Oxford: Oxford University Press, 1955.

Wright, Neil, ed. *The Historia Regum Britanniae of Geoffrey of Monmouth I: Bern, Burger-bibliothetk, MS 568: II The First Varient Version, A Critical Edition.* Cambridge: D. S. Brewer, 1984; 1988.

Secondary Sources

Albano, Robert A. *Middle English Historiography*. New York: Peter Lang, 1993.

Andrew, Malcolm. "The Fall of Troy in *Sir Gawain and the Green Knight* and *Troilus and Criseyde*. In *The European Tragedy of Troilus*. ed. Piero Boitani, 75–93. Oxford: Clarendon, 1989.

Archibald, Elizabeth. "The Flight from Incest: Two Classical Precursors of the Constance Theme." *Chaucer Review* 20.4 (1986): 259–72.

Atkinson, Clarissa W. *The Oldest Vocation: Christian Motherhood in the Middle Ages*. Ithaca: Cornell University Press, 1991.

Auerbach, Erich. *Mimesis: The Representation of Reality in Western Literature*. Translated by Willard R. Trask. Princeton: Princeton University Press, 1968.

Bell, Susan Groag. "Medieval Women Book Owners: Arbiters of Lay Piety and Ambassadors of Culture." *Signs*. 7 (1982): 742–68.

Bergren, Anne L. T. "Language and the Female in Early Greek Thought." *Arethusa* 16 (1983): 69–95.

Biddick, Kathleen. "Genders, Bodies, Borders: Technologies of the Visible." *Speculum* 68 (1993): 389–418.

Blacker, Jean. *The Faces of Time: Portrayal of the Past in Old French and Latin Historical Narrative of the Anglo-Norman Regnum*. Austin: University of Texas Press, 1994.

———. "Transformations of a Theme: The Depoliticization of the Arthurian World in the *Roman de Brut*." In *The Arthurian Tradition: Essays in Convergence*, ed. Mary Flowers Braswell and John Bugge, 54–74. Birmingham: University of Alabama Press, 1988.

Bloch, R. Howard. *Etymologies and Genealogies: A Literary Anthropology of the French Middle Ages*. Chicago: University of Chicago Press, 1983.

Bloomfield, Morton. "The *Man of Law's Tale*: A Tragedy of Victimization and a Christian Comedy." *PMLA* 87 (1972): 384–90.

Boots, John P. "Parataxis and Politics: Meaning and the Social Utility of Middle English Romances." In *A Humanist's Legacy: Essays in Honor of John Christian Bale*, ed. Dennis M. Jones, 3–10. Decorah, IA: Luther College, 1990.

Bracken, Christopher. "Constance and the Silkweavers: Working Women and Colonial Fantasy in Chaucer's *Man of Law's Tale*." *Princeton Journal of Women, Gender, and Culture* 8.1 (1994): 13–39.

Brandt, William J. *The Shape of Medieval History: Studies in Modes of Perception*. New Haven: Yale University Press, 1966.

Breisach, Ernst. *Historiography: Ancient, Medieval, and Modern*. Chicago: University of Chicago Press, 1983.

Brie, Friedrich W. D. *Geschichte und Quellen der mittelenglischen Prosa-chronick "The Brute of England" oder "The Chronicles of England."* Marburg: N. G. Elwert'sche Verlagsbuchhandlung, 1905.

Brooke, Christopher. "Geoffrey of Monmouth as a Historian." In *Church and Government in the Middle Ages*, ed. Christopher Brooke, D. Luscombe, G. Martin, and D. Owen, 77–91. Cambridge: Cambridge University Press, 1976.

Bynum, Caroline Walker. *Holy Feast and Holy Fast: The Religious Significance of Food to Medieval Women.* Berkeley: University of California Press, 1987.

Chibnall, Marjorie. *The Empress Matilda: Queen Consort, Queen Mother, and Lady of the English.* Oxford: Blackwell, 1991.

Clark, Cecily. "The Narrative Mode of the *Anglo-Saxon Chronicle* before the Conquest." In *England before the Conquest: Studies in Honor of Dorothy Whitelock.* ed. Peter Clemoes and Katherine Hughes. Cambridge: Cambridge University Press, 1971.

Clark, S. L. and Julian N. Wasserman. "Constance as Romance and Folk Heroine in Chaucer's *Man of Law's Tale.*" *Rice University Studies* 64 (1978): 13–24.

———. "Gawain's Anti-Feminism Reconsidered." *JRMMRA* 6 (1995): 57–70.

Correale, Robert M. "Chaucer's Manuscript of Nicholas Trevet's *Les Cronicles.* *Chaucer Review* 25.3 (1991): 238–65.

———. "Gower's Source Manuscript of Nicholas Trevet's *Les Cronicles.*" In *John Gower: Recent Readings*, ed. R. F. Yeager, 133–57. Kalamazoo, MI: Western Michigan University, 1989.

Crane, Susan. *Insular Romance: Politics, Faith, and Culture in Anglo-Norman and Middle English Literature.* Berkeley: University of California Press, 1986.

David, Alfred. "Gawain and Aeneas." *English Studies* 49.4 (August 1968): 402–09.

———. "The Man of Law vs. Chaucer: A Case in Poetics." *PMLA* 82 (1967): 217–25.

Dawson, Robert B. "Custance in Context: Rethinking the Protagonist of the *Man of Law's Tale.*" *Chaucer Review* 26.3 (1992): 293–308.

Dean, Ruth J. "The Manuscripts of Nicholas Trevet's Anglo- Norman Chronicles." *Medievalia et Humanistica* 14 (1962): 95–105.

———. "Nicholas Trevet, Historian." In *Medieval Learning and Literature: Essays Presented to Richard William Hunt*, ed. J. J. G. Alexander and M. T. Gibson, 328–52. Oxford: Clarendon Press, 1976.

Delany, Sheila. "Womanliness in the *Man of Law's Tale.*" *Chaucer Review* 9.1 (1974): 63–71.

Delasanta, Rodney. "And of Great Reverence: Chaucer's Man of Law." *Chaucer Review* 5.4 (1971): 288–310.

De Lauretis, Teresa. "Desire in Narrative," in her *Alice Doesn't: Feminism, Semiotics, Cinema*. Bloomington, IN: Indiana University Press, 1984.

Dinshaw, Carolyn. "The Man of Law and Its 'Abhomynacions.'" In *Chaucer's Sexual Poetics*. Madison, WI: University of Wisconsin, 1989.

Donoghue, Daniel and Bruce Mitchell. "Parataxis and Hypotaxis: A Review of Some Terms Used for Old English Syntax." *Neuphilologische Mitteilungen* 93.2 (1992): 163–83.

Dor, Julliette. "From the Crusading Virago to the Polysemous Virgin: Chaucer's Constance." In *A Wife There Was*. Liege, Belgium: Universite de Liege, 1992. 129–40.

Duby, Georges. *The Chivalrous Society*. Translated by Cynthia Postan. Berkeley: University of California Press, 1977.

———. *The Knight, the Lady, and the Priest: The Making of Modern Marriage in Medieval France*. Translated by Barbara Bray. New York: Pantheon Books, 1983.

Durling, Nancy Vine. "Translation and Innovation in the *Roman de Brut*." In *Medieval Translators and their Craft*, ed. Jeanette Beer, 248–74. *Studies in Medieval Culture* 25 Medieval Institute Publications. Kalamazoo, MI: Western Michigan University Press, 1989.

Ferrante, Joan. *To the Glory of her Sex: Women's Roles in the Composition of Medieval Texts*. Bloomington: Indiana University Press, 1997.

Fisher, Sheila. "Leaving Morgan Aside: Women, History, and Revisionism in *Sir Gawain and the Green Knight*. In *The Passing of Arthur: New Essays in Arthurian Tradition*, ed. Christopher Baswell and William Sharpe, 129–51. New York: Garland, 1988.

Flint, Valerie I. J. "The *Historia regum Britanniae* of Geoffrey of Monmouth: Parody and its Purpose: A Suggestion." *Speculum* 54.3 (July 1979): 447–68.

Fradenburg, Louise Olga. ed. "Introduction: Rethinking Queenship." In *Women and Sovereignty*. Edinburgh: Edinburgh University Press, 1992. 1–13.

Fradenburg, Louise O., with Carla Freccero. "The Pleasures of History." *Gay and Lesbian Quarterly* 1 (1995): 371–84.

Fries, Maureen. "Boethian Themes and Tragic Structure in Geoffrey of Monmouth's *Historia Regum Britanniae*." In *The Arthurian Tradition: Essays in Convergence*, ed. Mary Flowers Braswell and John Bugge, 29–42. Tuscaloosa: University of Alabama Press, 1988.

Fuss, Diana. *Essentially Speaking: Feminism, Nature, and Difference*. New York: Routledge, 1989.

Gaunt, Simon. *Gender and Genre in Medieval French Literature*. Cambridge: Cambridge University Press, 1995.

Gertz, Sunhee Kim. "*Translatio studii et imperii*: Sir Gawain as Literary Critic." *Semiotica* 63 1/2 (1987): 185–203.

Goyne, Jo. "Parataxis and Causality in the Tale of Sir Launcelot Du Lake." *Quondam et Futurus: A Journal of Arthurian Interpretations* 2.4 (Winter 1992): 38–48.

Gransden, Antonia. *Historical Writing in England, c. 550-c. 1307.* Ithaca: Cornell University Press, 1974.

———. *Historical Writing in England, c. 1307- 1600.* Ithaca: Cornell University Press, 1986.

Guerin, M. Victoria. "The King's Sin: The Origins of the David-Arthur Parallel." In *The Passing of Arthur: New Essays in Arthurian Tradition*, ed. Christopher Baswell and William Sharpe, 15–30. New York: Garland, 1988.

Hanks, Thomas. "*Emare*: An Influence on the *Man of Law's Tale.*" *Chaucer Review* 18.2 (1983): 182–86.

Hanning, Robert W. *The Individual in Twelfth-Century Romance.* New Haven: Yale University Press, 1977.

———. *The Vision of History in Early Britain from Gildas to Geoffrey of Monmouth.* New York: Columbia University Press, 1966.

Hay, Denys. *Annalists and Historians: Western Historiography from the Eighth to the Eighteenth Centuries.* London: Methuen, 1977.

Hendrix, Laurel L. "'Pennannce profytable': The Currency of Custance in Chaucer's *Man of Law's Tale.*" *Exemplaria* 6.1 (Spring 1994): 141–66.

Heng, Geraldine. "Cannibalism, the First Crusade, and the Genesis of Medieval Romance." *Differences: A Journal of Feminist Cultural Studies* 10.1 (Spring 1998): 98–174.

———. "Feminine Knots and the Other in *Sir Gawain and the Green Knight.*" *PMLA* 106.3 (May 1991): 500–14.

Herlihy, David. *Medieval Households.* Cambridge, MA: Harvard University Press, 1985.

Homans, Margaret. "Feminist Criticism and Theory: The Ghost of Creusa." *Yale Journal of Criticism* 1 (1987–88): 153–82.

Ingham, Patricia Clare. *Sovereign Fantasies: Arthurian Romance and the Making of Britain.* Philadelphia: University of Pennsylvania Press, 2001.

Ingledew, Francis. "The Book of Troy and the Genealogical Construction of History: The Case of Geoffrey of Monmouth's *Historia regum Britanniae.*" *Speculum* 69 (July 1994): 665–704.

Jambeck, Karen K. "Patterns of Women's Literary Patronage: England, 1200-ca. 1475." In *The Cultural Patronage of Medieval Women*, ed. June Hall McCash, 228–65. Athens: University of Georgia Press, 1996.

Johnson, William C., Jr. *"The Man of Law's Tale*: Aesthetics and Christianity in Chaucer." *Chaucer Review* 16.3 (1982): 201–21.

Jucker, Andreas H. "Between Hypotaxis and Parataxis: Clauses of Reason in *Ancrene Wisse.*" In *Historical English Syntax*, ed. Dieter Kastovsky, 203–20. Berlin: Mouton de Gruyter, 1991.

Kennedy, Edward Donald. ed. *Chronicles and Other Historical Writing.* Vol. 8, *Manual of the Writings in Middle English, 1050–1500*, ed. Albert E. Hartung. Hamden, CT: Archon Books, 1989.

Knight, Stephen. "'So Great a King: Geoffrey of Monmouth's *Historia regum Britanniae.*" In *Arthurian Literature and Society.* London: Macmillan, 1983. 38–67.

Kolve, V. A. *Chaucer and the Imagery of Narrative.* Stanford: Stanford University Press, 1984.

Krishna, Valerie. "Parataxis, Formulaic Density, and Thrift in the *Alliterative Morte Arthure.*" *Speculum* 57.1 (1982): 63–83.

Krueger, Roberta L. *Women Readers and the Ideology of Gender in Old French Verse Romance.* Cambridge: Cambridge University Press, 1993.

Legge, M. Dominica. *Anglo-Norman Literature and Its Background.* Oxford: Clarendon Press, 1963.

Leicester, Marshall H., Jr. *The Disenchanted Self: Representing the Subject in the "Canterbury Tales."* Berkeley: University of California Press, 1990.

Lepick, Julie Ann. "History and Story: The End and Ending of *La Mort le Roi Artu.*" *Michigan Academician* 12.4 (Spring 1980): 517–26.

Liuzza, Roy. "Names, Reputation, and History in *Sir Gawain and the Green Knight.*" *Essays in Medieval Studies: Proceedings of the Illinois Medieval Association* 6 (1989): 41–56.

Lyon, Bryce. *A Constitutional and Legal History of Medieval England.* New York: Harper and Row, 1960.

Margherita, Gayle. "Father Aeneas or Morgan the Goddess." In *The Romance of Origins: Language and Sexual Difference in Middle English Literature.* Philadelphia: University of Pennsylvania Press, 1994. 129–51.

Matheson, Lister M. "Historical Prose." In *Middle English Prose*, ed. A. S. G. Edwards, 209–28. New Brunswick: Rutgers University Press, 1984.

———. "King Arthur and the Medieval English Chronicles." In *King Arthur Through the Ages*, ed. Valerie M. Lagorio and Mildred Leake Day, 1:248–74. New York: Garland, 1990.

———. "The Middle English Prose *Brut*: A Location List of the Manuscripts and Early Printed Editions." *Analytical & Enumerative Bibliography* 3 (1979): 254–66.

McCash, June Hall, ed. *The Cultural Patronage of Medieval Women*. Athens: University of Georgia Press, 1996.

McCracken, Peggy. "The Body Politic and the Queen's Adulterous Body in French Romance." In *Feminist Approaches to the Body in Medieval Literature*, ed. Linda Lomperis and Sarah Stanbury, 38–64. Philadelphia: University of Pennsylvania Press, 1993.

———— "Engendering Sacrifice: Blood, Lineage, and Infanticide in Old French Literature." *Speculum* 77 (2002): 55–75.

Nicholson, Peter. "Chaucer Borrows from Gower: The Sources of the *Man of Law's Tale*." In *Chaucer and Gower: Difference, Mutuality, and Exchange*, ed. R. F. Yeager, 85–99. Victoria, BC: University of Victoria, 1991.

————. "The *Man of Law's Tale*: What Chaucer Really Owed to Gower." *Chaucer Review* 26.2 (1991): 153–74.

Ong, Walter J. "Latin Language Study as a Renaissance Puberty Rite." *Studies in Philology* 56 (1956): 103–24.

————. *Orality and Literacy: The Technologizing of the Word*. London: Methuen & Co, 1982.

Parsons, John Carmi. ed. *Medieval Queenship*. New York: St. Martin's Press, 1993.

————. "Of Queens, Courts, and Books: Reflections on the Literary Patronage of Thirteenth-Century Plantagenet Queens." In *The Cultural Patronage of Medieval Women*, ed. June Hall McCash, 175–201. Athens: University of Georgia Press, 1996.

————. "Ritual and Symbol in the English Medieval Queenship to 1500." In *Women and Sovereignty*, ed. Louise Olga Fradenburg, 60–77. Edinburgh: Edinburgh University Press, 1992.

Parsons, John Carmi and Bonnie Wheeler, eds. *Medieval Mothering*. New York: Garland, 1996.

Partner, Nancy F. *Serious Entertainments: The Writing of History in Twelfth-Century England*. Chicago: University of Chicago Press, 1977.

Patterson, Lee. "The Romance of History and the Alliterative *Morte Arthure*." In *Negotiating the Past: The Historical Understanding of Medieval Literature*. Madison, WI: University of Wisconsin Press, 1987.

Pratt, Robert. "Chaucer and *Les Cronicles* of Nicholas Trevet." In *Studies in Language, Literature and Culture of the Middle Ages and Later*, ed. E. Bagby Atwood and Archibald A. Hill, 303–11. Austin: University of Texas Press, 1969.

Raybin, David. "Custance and History: Woman as Outsider in Chaucer's *Man of Law's Tale*." *Studies in the Age of Chaucer* 12 (1990): 65–84.

Riley, Denise. "Does A Sex Have a History?" In *Feminism and History*, ed. Joan Wallach Scott, 17–33. Oxford: Oxford University Press, 1996.

Roddy, Kevin. "Mythic Sequence in the *Man of Law's Tale*." *Journal of Medieval and Renaissance Studies* 10.1 (1980): 1–22.

Rubin, Gayle. "The Traffic in Women." In *Toward an Anthropology of Women*, ed. Rayna R. Reiter, 157–210. New York: Monthly Press Review, 1975.

Russell, J. Stephen. "Dido, Emily, and Constance: Femininity and Subversion in the Mature Chaucer." *Medieval Perspectives* 1.1 (Spring 1986), ed. Pedro F. Campa, Charles W. Conwell, Robert J. Vallier. 65–73.

Scheps, Walter. "Chaucer's *Man of Law* and the Tale of Constance." *PMLA* 89 (1974): 285–95.

Schibanoff, Susan. "Worlds Apart: Orientalism, Antifeminism, and Heresy in Chaucer's *Man of Law's Tale*." *Exemplaria* 8.1 (Spring 1996): 59–96.

Schlauch, Margaret. *Chaucer's Constance and Accursed Queens*. New York: New York University Press, 1927; Reprint, New York: Godian Press, 1969.

———. "The Man of Law's Tale." In *Sources and Analogues of Chaucer's "Canterbury Tales*, ed. W. F. Bryan and G. Dempster, 155–206. Chicago: University of Chicago Press, 1941.

Scott, Joan Wallach. *Gender and the Politics of History*. New York: Columbia University Press, 1988.

Shadis, Miriam. "Piety, Politics, and Power: The Patronage of Leonor of England and Her Daughters Berenguela of Leon and Blanche of Castile." In *The Cultural Patronage of Medieval Women*, ed. June Hall McCash, 202–27. Athens: University of Georgia Press, 1996.

Sheingorn, Pamela. "Appropriating the Holy Kinship: Gender and Family History." In *Interpreting Cultural Symbols: Saint Anne in Late Medieval Society*, ed. Kathleen Ashley and Pamela Sheingorn, 169–98. Athens: University of Georgia Press, 1990.

———. "The Holy Kinship: The Ascendency of Matriliny in Sacred Genealogy of the Fifteenth Century." *Thought* 64.254 (September 1989): 268–86.

Shoaf, R. A. "'Unwemmed Custance': Circulation, Property, and Incest in the *Man of Law's Tale*" *Exemplaria* 2.1 (March 1990): 287–302.

Shwartz, Susan M. "The Founding and Self-Betrayal of Britain: An Augustinian Approach to Geoffrey of Monmouth's *Historia Regum Britanniae*." *Medievalia et Humanistica: Studies in Medieval and Renaissance Culture*. ns 10 (1981): 33–54.

Silverstein, Theodore. "*Sir Gawain*, Dear Brutus, and Britain's Fortune Founding: A Study in Comedy and Convention." *Modern Philology* 62 (February 1963): 189–206.

Speigel, Gabrielle. "Genealogy: Form and Function in Medieval Historical Narrative." *History and Theory* 22 (1983): 45–53.

———. *Romancing the Past: The Rise of Vernacular Prose Historiography in Thirteenth-Century France.* Berkeley: University of California Press, 1993.

Stock, Brian. *The Implications of Literacy: Written Language and Models of Interpretation in the Eleventh and Twelfth Centuries.* Princeton: Princeton University Press, 1983.

Tatlock, J. S. P. *The Legendary History of Britain: Geoffrey of Monmouth's "Historia Regum Britaniae" and its Early Vernacular Versions.* Berkeley: University of California Press, 1950; Reprint, New York: Gordian Press, 1974.

Taylor, John. *English Historical Literature in the Fourteenth Century.* Oxford: Clarendon Press, 1987.

———. "The French 'Brut' and the Reign of Edward II." *English Historical Review* 77 (1987): 423–37.

Tolhurst, Fiona. "The Britons as Hebrews, Normans, and Romans: Geoffrey of Monmouth's British Epic and Reflections of Empress Matilda." *Arthuriana* 8.4 (Winter 1998): 69–87.

———. "Geoffrey of Monmouth's *Historia Regum Britannie* and the Critics" *Arthuriana* 8.4 (Winter 1998). Special issue on Geoffrey of Monmouth.

Tyson, Diana B. "Patronage of French Vernacular History Writers in the Twelfth and Thirteenth Centuries." *Romania* 100 (1979): 180–222.

Warren, Michelle R. *History on the Edge: Excalibur and the Borders of Britain, 1100–1300.* Minneapolis: University of Minnesota Press, 2000.

Wasserman, Julian and Robert Blanch. "Gawain's Anti-Feminism: From Gollancz and Tolkien to the Millennium." *Medieval Perspectives* 15 (Fall 2000): 21–33.

Waswo, Richard. "The History that Literature Makes." *New Literary History: A Journal of Theory and Interpretation* 19.3 (Spring 1988): 541–64.

———. "Our Ancestors, The Trojans: Inventing Cultural Identity in the Middle Ages." *Exemplaria* 7.2 (Fall 1995): 269–90.

Weisberg, David. "Telling Stories About Constance: Framing and Narrative Strategy in the *Canterbury Tales.*" *Chaucer Review* 27.1 (1992): 45–64.

Wetherbee, Winthrop. "Constance and the World in Chaucer and Gower." In *John Gower: Recent Readings,* ed. R. F. Yeager, 65–93. Kalamazoo, MI: Western Michigan University, 1989.

Wheeler, Bonnie. "Romance and Parataxis and Malory." *Arthurian Literature* 13 (1993): 109–32.

White, Hayden. "The Value of Narrativity in the Representation of Reality." In *The Content of the Form: Narrative Discourse and Historical Representation.* Baltimore: Johns Hopkins University Press, 1987. 1–25.

Wynn, Phillip. "The Conversion Story in Nicholas Trevet's "Tale of Constance." *Viator* 13 (1984): 259–74.

INDEX

Studies in the Humanities

Edited by Guy Mermier

The Studies in the Humanities series welcomes manuscripts discussing various aspects of the humanities. The series' emphasis is on medieval and Renaissance literatures with a focus on Western civilizations and cultures. Submissions dealing with linguistics, history, politics, or sociology within the same time frame and geographical bounds are also encouraged. Manuscripts may be submitted in English, French, or Italian. The preferred style manual is the MLA Handbook (1995).

For additional information about this series or for the submission of manuscripts, please contact:

Dr. Heidi Burns
Peter Lang Publishing, Inc.
P.O. Box 1246
Bel Air, MD 21014-1246

To order other books in this series, please contact our Customer Service Department:

(800) 770-LANG (within the U.S.)
(212) 647-7706 (outside the U.S.)
(212) 647-7707 FAX

or browse online by series:

WWW.PETERLANGUSA.COM